# Parenting: Where Are We Going Wrong?

By Manmohan Chopra

Copyright 2014 by Manmohan Chopra

ISBN: 978-0-69233-093-7

# Table of Contents

# **Preface**

We are not the same as we were a few decades back. Society over all has changed. Subtle changes always happen, but lately with these changes, now we have become greedier, more materialistic, egoistic, mean, and self-centered. We do not care for our fellow human beings the way we used to. When we are driving, we cut others off to go ahead and we do not let anyone pass.

That is, as soon as you give an indication you want to change lanes, the person far behind in the other lane might race up next to you and start driving ever so casually. What does he get by doing that? Maybe just a little bit of elation that he did not let you get ahead of him, that's all.

And a similar scenario occurs in the workplace. Coworkers do not think twice before stabbing someone from behind to get ahead. Our thirst for money and power causes us to lose sight of others and think solely about ourselves and what it takes for us to win the race.

In a word, we are getting mean in our daily life.

There is so much anger building up in us, especially in the younger generation, that it explodes with the smallest spark, sometimes even without a trigger. For example, everyone seems to want to sue someone else on a small pretext. This comes from the parents and society, as we do not think twice before uttering those words: I am going to sue you! And sometimes there is not even a pretext. Someone sues another person just for money or some gratification we can't identify.

Once upon a time, when you smiled at someone, you received a reciprocal smile. In the past, people were friendlier and treated each other with respect. People were eager to help each other.

It used to be bad manners if an older person was standing while riding a bus and we were sitting. There are people who would right away get up and offer their seat to the seniors, but unfortunately, most people would just turn their eyes away now as if they do not even see that person standing there.

Why is this culture of friendliness, caring, and helping others fading away as time progresses? Maybe it was because we were raised that way, taught from the cradle to be selfish and mean.

People of the current generation in particular are becoming restless, impatient, mean, aggressive, and disrespectful. They expect instant gratification for anything and everything. They could care less for anything but themselves.

It seems that a disaster is heading our way and we are failing to see it. But I don't want to believe an utterly negative future awaits us because there is always a silver lining. We still may have some hope, as there are more honest and ethical people in this world than people with no values.

If this were not the case, then I would hold out no hope at all for our culture, but we still see cases such as a taxi driver turning in a wallet full of money to the police so it can be returned to the rightful owner. The driver could have kept the money and no one would have known, and maybe he could have paid his bills for two or three months with that money. But he didn't! His actions show us the honesty he may have received from his upbringing. His parents may have shown him the right path and taught him about right and wrong.

Because we see more negative stories every day than positive stories as this one, the positive stories come as a fresh blossom in our day.

When I started writing this book, I searched libraries and the internet for books and articles about why we are seeing a big behavioral change in the children of today. I wanted to find out some books on Parenting. Unfortunately, I could not find anything that covered the whole subject. I found that the books written on parenting so far covered only certain topics regarding the issue. These books were written by very well respected experts and writers, and hats off to these writers who covered the important issues they did and for trying to teach the masses about those issues. However, because of this lack of information in one book about the entire issue, I tried to cover as much as possible.

Throughout the book, you may notice some repetition of messages across different subjects. The reason I did that was to make those messages stay with the reader so they can be passed on to our next generation. The whole idea is to educate ourselves first and then educate our kids about the ramifications of all these issues. And I have found that a parent better know what he or she is talking about in our day and age, which is not like when we were growing up. We would not question our parents if told to do something, for example, but today's kids want a reason for everything—and there is nothing wrong in that. But if you cannot give a reason for something, they will not take what you say seriously.

It took me a while to complete this book, and I am thankful to few people who encouraged me to keep going. First and foremost, I am thankful to my parents and want to dedicate my book to Late Krishan Kumar and Brij Rani Chopra, and to my grandparents Late Shiv Nath and Kaushalya Rani Chopra who always taught us good things in life in a very subtle manner. My father was a wise man. He taught us to be humble in life and to keep our feet firmly on ground. He led his life based on a theory of high morals and humility. He was a very well respected gentleman among the people who knew him. At a given time of his career, he got into the circle of some top actors, directors, producers of Indian cinema (Bollywood), and he made friends with them, but he was never star struck by them. He treated every person the same.

My mother, though not literate, was a very good administrator. She had a knack for delegating work in a very nice and simple way. She was energetic and taught us not to be lazy. My grandfather was a very simple and honest person, and my noble grandmother showed us a path to be humble, God-fearing, and respectful to others. Though not formally educated, she was a wise lady and people used to seek her advice on different matters. I was blessed to have been raised in a family where I could learn so much from everyone around me.

I would like to thank my wife, Hema, for her support in helping me complete this book. I am also thankful to both my sons, who gave me some insights for the book and helped me in my business, so that I could complete this project.

During my research, I came into contact with experts in their respective fields, and I want to thank them from the core of my heart for their help and support.

I am thankful to:

- Michael Shulman, Public Affairs Specialist (American Psychology Association) for allowing me to use certain content from their site.

- Dr. Larry D. Rosen, PhD (Professor, Keynote Speaker, Research Consultant), California State University, Dominguez Hills, for his valuable input from his research.

- Dr. Kaveri Subrahmanyam, PhD, Child Psychologist, Professor, California State University of Los Angeles.

- Dr. Stephanie Mihalas, PhD, Child Psychologist.

I am also thankful to Vandana Kumar and Juan Campos, both teachers, and my friend Dr. Gurdip Flora for their help and valuable insight and input for this book. I would also like to thank the writers on various subtopics within the issue for their insight.

I do not consider myself close to the equal of those great writers, but I have tried my best to put certain things I have learned in my life into this book in a concise way along with as much insight as I could find on the topic. I will be thankful to God if, through this book, even just one person can benefit.

# Chapter 1: Parenting – Where Are We Going WRONG?

### Actual Scenario #1:

I was sitting outside a hospital talking on the phone, distracted by about a six-year old child who was constantly hovering around me and yelling at no one in particular. I did not notice that his father was sitting there too until, all of a sudden, this little boy went to his father and slapped him on his face. I was stunned and completely forgot my conversation. However, what surprised me even more was to see his father's reaction to this. Guess what? He did nothing to stop his son let alone to discipline him or even tell him that it was very inappropriate to hit someone like that. The son again hovered around and yelled, and the father continued just sitting there, doing nothing in particular. Thinking about it, I believe that the little boy and his dad were accustomed to that outrageous behavior. It was just normal to them.

### Actual scenario # 2:

I was taking a walk in the evening when I noticed a lady sitting in her parked car. She was busy talking on her cell phone, clearly oblivious of the fact that her young daughter of around four years, who was apparently bored, was banging hard on the side glass pane of the car with another cell phone. The mother was not even worried nor did she seem to care if something happened to her daughter. Talking on the phone was more important to her than anything else at the time. Apparently, she did not even know what her daughter was doing.

### Actual Scenario # 3:

As I was walking on a sidewalk, I saw a small girl about to throw a stone at the cars parked across the street. But then she stopped.

I stood there motionless and heard that girl say to her friend, "No, I won't throw the stone because my dad's car is also parked there."

The girl *only* stopped because her dad's car was parked there, too. She was not concerned about damaging other cars. The most important point in this story was that her mother was standing right next to her and she did not say anything to her daughter to correct her. She did not tell her that it is wrong to damage others' property.

**Actual Scenario # 4:**

"100 Students Ejected from New York to Atlanta Flight"

Associated Press news report on Yahoo, June 5, 2013.

A group of about 100 high school students traveling from New York to Atlanta were thrown off a flight, along with their chaperones, after the pilot and crew lost patience with some kids who wouldn't sit down and put away their cell phones.

AirTrans' parent company, Southwest Airlines, said in a statement that flight attendants asked passengers several times to take their seats and put their mobile devices away. The airline said that when some didn't comply, the captain repeated the request. When that didn't work either, the whole group of students was ordered to disembark for safety reasons, the airline said.

The flight was delayed for about 45 minutes while the students filed out of the Boeing 737, which seats about 137 people, leaving the plane mostly empty".

Now, let us read some of the comments of readers, which appeared under this news:

**Douglas**

I am a teacher and it is like pulling teeth to get kids to put away cell phones and sometimes, even parents will call their children on their cells and they know the kid is in class!

**Bud**

Drove a school bus for 3 1/2 years and know how this stuff can happen. Have driven on field trips where the kids were acting like morons and the teacher chaperones just sat there and said nothing. Many parents who think that their children are angels would be amazed at their behavior when mommy and daddy aren't around.

**Menanny**

We are raising a generation of selfish individuals who think they are entitled. I say to the parents - *STOP IT NOW*! Raise them like you should - they are not your friends, they are your children.

## Actual Scenario # 5:

"Looting on a Grand Scale by Teenagers: 16 Teens Arrested After Vacant La Habra Heights mansion in California is trashed"

*Los Angeles Times* (Late Extra edition), December 12, 2013 (excerpts)

"In a case that seems a cross between the *Bling Ring Celebrity Burglars* and another installment of *The Hangover*, sheriff's officials arrested 16 people on December 11, 2013 in connection with a mansion party where guests walked off with medieval armor, scuba gear, Armani suits and – the *piece de resistance* – a mounted snow leopard worth $ 250,000. More than 100 people were estimated to have attended the party held at a vacant, fully furnished La Habra Heights mansion on the night of November 23. The damage and thievery amount to at least $1 million, and Sheriff Lee Baca said the severity of the damage was so great that it ranked as one of the worst juvenile crimes he has seen. Thirteen of the arrested were juveniles – three girls and 10 boys between the ages 15 to 17 years. What's funny is that when the teen who stole the mounted snow leopard was told that it was worth more than $ 250,000, the teen asked, "How many zeroes is that?"

Some of the suspects essentially identified themselves by posting "selfies" with their loot to social media accounts to brag about their haul, officials said. The photos aided detectives' efforts to find the suspects. Those who are arrested appeared to be "kids of means" Sheriff Baca said. The teens face a range of charges, from trespassing to grand theft, which carries a possible jail sentence."

*For people who have not heard about the* Bling Ring Celebrity Burglars – *these were a bunch of teens supposedly from wealthy families who, along with two other men, allegedly got into celebrities' homes such as Megan Fox, Lindsey Lohan, and Paris Hilton and stole jewelry worth millions of dollars a few years back.*

10

## Scenario # 6:

Imagine going to a store to shop for some clothes. For you it is fun looking at the new clothes and trying them on. However, it is not fun for the kids to tag along. They are bored, and to get rid of this boredom, they start doing unimaginable things like pulling clothes from the hangers and running in the aisles. In fact, many times when mothers are shopping, they don't even know where their kids are in the store. Have you ever imagined how much extra work and headache is it for the store clerks to put those clothes back on the hangers and arrange everything that your kids have strewn all over the place? Do you think they love this extra work? What would you think of such a child's behavior, and his or her parent's lack of parenting skills, if you were in that clerk's shoes? As parents it is our duty to teach the kids not to act like that. If our kid pulls something from the shelf, we should ask him to put it back the way it was. If we do not guide them, it will become a habit in them, and they will even do those kinds of things at home too.

And have you noticed the changes in kids' health in the last few decades? Do you remember how the kids used to look 20 or 30 years back and how do they look now? Not only are more kids now days caring less about others, disrespectful, unethical, lazy, and so but they are getting bigger, even obese, as their eating habits are distorted.

Whose fault do you think it is?

And have you ever noticed a young kid back-talking an adult or saying cuss words to the teacher or someone else older, showing no respect whatsoever? Unfortunately, most people tend to just ignore such behavior even in their own children.

Perhaps some of you might be thinking about now, "Well, my kid sometimes behaves in a similar way to one or more of these examples." If that is the case, it is time to educate your child.

It is sometimes very hard to discern what is right or wrong, and in fact it is not my intent here to find right or wrong but to find a little common sense and a happy medium as regards how we can raise children. My hope is that we can change how children are raised

11

currently so that we as parents don't regret tomorrow, but also so that all of us as a community or as a nation don't regret what our community or nation has become.

Thinking about this issue and the following points was what led me to write this book:

- Are we alienating our kids?

- Are we giving kids the right direction?

- Are we trying hard to give them the right education?

- Are we teaching them the right ethics?

- Are we giving them the culture we inherited from our grandparents?

- Are we taking the right steps to raise our kids?

In fact, we are living in a society in which we are slowly separating from each other, becoming detached from our families and our old values and culture. We are spending more time on computers than with our kids. Kids are spending more time on their phones, playing video games, and searching the internet than with their parents. To answer some of the questions noted above: children are not getting the right direction, education, moral values, and civic sense like we use to. They are learning wrong things. They are becoming more destructive. Every day we hear the horror stories of kids and teens getting killed in gang wars. We see kids taking guns into a school and shooting innocent people. We see more graffiti in our neighborhood, and when looking at some of it wonder how a child can be so artistic, intelligent, and energetic and yet their intelligence and energy is being wasted.

**Why is this happening?**

**It is mainly because of us adults, who should be showing the way to their children but aren't.**

Of course, this will sound shocking because no one wants to take the blame and everyone thinks they are raising their kids in the best possible way. I am not trying to offend anyone here, but let us reflect on our behavior to determine what we are doing and if it is right. Ask yourself the following questions:

- Do we take time to talk to our kids everyday about their issues, problems, etc.?

- Do we care how much time they spend on the phones and watching television and what kind of channels/programs they watch?

- Do we know what kind of people they associate with?

- Do we teach them about the value of money?

- Do we teach them to respect other people?

- Do we ask them about their homework, teachers, school, progress, etc.?

- Do we genuinely ask them about their aspirations, goals, and what they want to become in life?

- Do we instill in them a basic civic sense?

- Do we guide them about the rights and the wrongs in life?

- Do we try to give them a direction to become successful in life?

- Do we counsel them in respect of different things in life?

Just to give kids shelter and food on their plates is not enough. We need to do much more than that if we want a better future for our kids. And after all a better future for your kids may bring a better future for you too for we all want our children to grow up to be responsible, self-reliant, contributors to the family and maybe our church and the community where we live—even to the nation as a whole.

Life is tough for all parents, but it is especially hard for single parents who have to take care of their job, cook, do the laundry, run errands, and make ends meet. They have the stress of dropping their kids at school on time, and then they go to work where, if they are late, the boss is going to yell at them. With a limited income, they have to worry about where to leave their too-young-yet-for-school kids as they go to their job. Sometimes, it is the job that gets sacrificed. Sometimes the single parents have to let a promotion go to another person, perhaps because it entails travel and they can't leave their children home alone.

Sacrifice.

Sacrifice..

and more Sacrifice…

It is amazing how some people singlehandedly beat the odds and do all the things they are required to do to raise their kids in a phenomenal way. It is definitely not an easy task, but with determination and hard work, they accomplish that goal.

However, regardless of whether they are a single parent or not, some parents do not take the very important role of parenting seriously and mess up the kids', as well as their own lives.

Although parenting is a hard subject, it is not even rocket science that it cannot be done right by a common person. In fact, life can be so much better if we take some simple steps from the very beginning and do parenting right.

Let us now check about some simple, but great ways, where we can make a big difference, as to how we raise our kids!

It is hard to say whether the right way to raise kids is an art form or a matter of common sense. How you go about raising your children in the best possible way also depends on your situation, needs, educational background, your own thinking, financial circumstances, family situation, and culture, etc. To begin with, living life with kids absolutely requires the right attitude. Without it, and up until the time you develop a good one, an unhealthy attitude about this business of being good parents will make things pretty tough, to say the least. A lot also depends as to how you were raised.

Overall our circumstances have changed much in the last few decades. In older times, not only were families bigger but we had grandparents, uncles and aunts, and cousins around us. The older and wiser people around us used to give proper guidance to the younger generation. If someone from the younger generation made a mistake, there were older people advising or even punishing them and thereby passing on their experience and knowledge to the younger generation. The older generation would also teach the younger the importance of camaraderie and helping each other, and with cousins living together, children learn a sense of sharing things and of enjoying doing things together. Helping each other in such an atmosphere comes automatically.

Vandana Kumar, a teacher, concurs with this. "Here, it is very important as to how they have been raised. It will be different for a kid raised amongst their cousins and relatives than for a kid raised solely. The kid raised with cousins or relatives would learn concepts of sharing and caring more easily. That child will also learn how to adjust to others. Well, it is really difficult in these times when we have the nuclear family concept. However, we can try inculcating those same values in our kids in their early lives so that they do not suffer with that issue when they grow up."

With the changes in socio economic conditions and the spread of urban areas, the old values of togetherness have slowly vanished. Now there are smaller families, and in fact families are getting yet smaller as people want their independence and do not want responsibilities. Lots of people shun the idea of marriage for they do not want to be bound by a relationship. And of course there is the increase in divorce and sex outside of marriage, which results in single parent families.

Single parents have to leave their child with a baby sitter in order to be able to work, and surveys have shown that most single parent families are driven towards poverty. Just imagine how hard it is to maintain a family if a person is working at a minimum wage job and then has to pay a big chunk of money to the baby sitter or to the school for that matter.

In the past, there was a family support system. If the parent had to go to work, there were grandparents at home taking care of the children. In the absence of the parents at home, the grandparents would tell the grandkids stories and teach them other important things. And as a result kids used to learn about their culture, respect, sharing, caring, and etc. I don't mean to suggest that there are only positive things associated with joint or bigger families, but it seems there are certainly more pros than cons.

Now we will look at what is important to raise children in the right way. We will go over these important elements to good parenting one by one in the following chapters.

# Chapter 2: Education

*Education is an investment, not an expense.*

"Live as if you were to die tomorrow. Learn as if you were to live forever." – Mahatma Gandhi.

"Education is the most powerful weapon which you can use to change the world." – Nelson Mandela.

Education is not only an investment in our children's future, affording them respect in society as well as a tool to build their future, but an investment in the community's and the country's future. It is only through education that our children will get good jobs such as doctors, scientists, and leaders; but education also empowers individual citizens and the nation as a whole. In fact, education is the foundation of any society.

However, getting an education is also a most basic thing in life and starts right from birth. In fact, in Judaism, the womb is the first critical environment for formation of the child; and likewise in Hinduism, it is said that education starts in the womb. As Swami Satchidananda, the spiritual Guru says: "The pregnant woman is the baby's first teacher. Her womb provides materials for the child's soul to build itself a physical body, and she molds her child's character by adding new impressions. Caring for a child's mind is more important than caring for his body. If an organ becomes diseased, another organ can be transplanted in its place, but you can never transplant the mind. And the mind is built up first by the mother. She can make it or break it."

Maharishi Mahesh Yogi agrees that the mother's role in the child's education begins when the child has yet to be born: "The heart of the mother determines the consciousness of the child." And Rousseau, although he might not agree that education begins prior to birth, agrees with the primacy of the mother as teacher: "Our earliest teacher is the mother."

So, if the mother is the first teacher of the child, then the role of the mother becomes all the more powerful and important. It becomes absolutely necessary for the mother to take care of herself beginning in the pregnancy phase.

The pregnant mother should do the following:

- Eat healthy.

- Think healthy.

- Keep away from all the vices, such as smoking, alcohol, gambling, drugs, etc.

- Read good literature and keep her thoughts positive.

American medical universities are doing research on the assertion that a child starts learning from the mother, his family, and the people around him even before he enters the world. So, we need to make sure that he starts learning good things from the very beginning and be careful as to what environment we give the child right from the start.

After the child is born, we need to teach kids the right things in life. The point is to start inculcating good things in the child at the right age and time. For example, at the very beginning stages of childhood, you should read your child good stories, which does three things for him. First, it amuses him and he starts the learning process. Second, it starts making your bond with your child stronger. Third, it starts giving him education about wrong and right at an early age. When your parents read you a story, you no doubt asked questions at the end of the story because you wanted to know the reason for the bad guy's actions or why it is bad to steal. In short, storytelling is a subtle way to educate your child at an early age, morally as well as intellectually.

However, the practice of parents reading to their children is waning. Presently, if the child is getting bored or is disturbed, to keep him busy the parent will hand over their smart phone so their children can play with it. These children are infants and toddlers! Imagine what happens next. As a child gets fascinated with the lights and colors, the child gets hooked to that device and does not want to leave it. You might have seen kids crying when that phone was taken away from them. Rather than placating a child with some electronic device that you must then take away, thereby disappointing him, why not read to him as your mother read to you. Your bond will grow stronger, as it did between you and your mother.

It is also of paramount importance that you are engaged in your child's learning throughout his life, and there should be no compromises here. Follow what he is learning every day, as just sending him to school is not enough. Make it fun for him, so the child starts loving school and looks forward to going to school every day. Kids are smart, but they do need our help in determining a path for their lives. Initially, we have to hold their tiny hands to show them a path, and once they see the path, then they can usually chart the path for themselves.

However, some kids need their elders' help for a longer time. In that case, you have to make sure to hold their hands and guide them until they start their career. Our duty is to show them the path and to make sure that they are going in a good direction. It is very easy to fall from the path and to go astray, stumbling into thorns such as drugs and violence. So we have to make sure that our kids are protected and that they learn from our experience so that their life is easier. Don't be afraid to tell them about your mistakes. It does not demean you. They will admire you even more if you tell them where you faltered in life so they know that you can be their guide to help them avoid those mistakes. In short, education also builds character and discipline in the kids.

And in the absence of this character and discipline building, kids are more likely to leave the path altogether and abandon their education. Today, whereas the parents in South Asian countries are putting lots of emphasis on their children's education, lots of kids are dropping out of high school in the US. Whereas South Asian parents make sure that their kids get a college degree, and in fact encourage their children to do much more than just get a college degree, the United States has to get skilled people from outside the country because of a lack of qualified job applicants.

Per a National Center for Education Statistics (NCES) report, on average 3.4 percent of students dropped out without completing high school in 2009. The estimated dropout rate by race was as follows: 2.4 percent for whites, 4.8 percent for African Americans, and 5.8 percent for Latinos. It is not just the parents who are to blame for the high dropout rates, of course, but also socio-economic issues, poor school attendance, poor grades, grade retention, and crime in a particular area.

Doctor Kaveri stated that a lot of higher level learning happens at school, but parents need to communicate these basic values to their kids: the importance of work, education, and respect for teachers. In fact, however, Vandana Kumar, a teacher, emphasizes the fact that children these days do not value education. Rather, they are satisfied with the fact that they can earn money in ways that do not involve education and so degrees do not matter to them. They concentrate on the present and do not see the value they might realize from an education ten years from now.

Juan Campos, Dean of Students at Francis Polytechnic Senior High in California, adds that parents often think it is the responsibility of the school to groom the kids. However, it is of utmost importance for both parents and teachers alike to reinforce the importance of education for their kids. If the parents lack this belief, it is difficult to teach this importance to their kids. In fact, a lot of parents these days are giving the wrong perception of education to their kids by belittling their teachers in front of the kids. They should instead emphasize that it is not teachers vs students in this relationship, but rather that teachers are there to assist students.

Educators are not the only teachers in kid's life. The first educators are their parents and family. If they learn negative things from the parents or family, there is a strong possibility that they are not going to heed to the positive things their teachers are trying to instill in them.

# Train them while they are still young

It is very important for parents to get involved when their children are quite young to guide them correctly regarding the importance of getting an education. When you catch them young and start counseling them for their future, they understand better and those lessons stay with them forever.

Start by reading stories to them when they are two or younger, which achieves two things. You are starting to connect with them by showing them your love. They respond by cuddling to you, and they start listening to you. Now they understand who is in command. They feel your thoughts, love, and compassion. They also start to learn to listen and start asking questions about the stories regarding right and wrong.

As they grow little older, along with buying toys for them, buy something educational for them as well so that they start learning different things. Kids are smart and pick things up easily because they are not yet afraid to make a mistake, and in fact do not know what a mistake is. You will be amazed at their brain, which is like a big sponge. It absorbs everything they see, experience, or are taught. So, it is very important that they are taught good things when they are young.

Lots of self-employed people, like small business owners, may say that they get so busy with their business and work that they do not have enough time to interact with their kids. Although it is understandable for the small business owner to have so much on their plate, I would argue that we can always make time for our kids. It is for them that we are working so hard in the first place. I have seen some small business owners bring their children to their shops after school, but it is rare that they spend their time constructively with them there. You will see the kids hanging outside the shops with their skateboards or small bicycles as their parents are working inside. The shops and businesses are not always busy. So, whenever you have free time, you can always call your kids and start teaching them about something of importance.

For instance, you can help them finish their homework, and then you and your children do not have to worry about it at home. This way they also learn how to use time more effectively. If they learn about time-management at an early age, they will not have issues later and you will not have complaints that they are just wasting their time when they grow older. But such interactions are not just about studies. You can teach them about money matters or your business, depending on their age.

Many parents out of necessity leave their kids at childcare centers when they go to work, but they should absolutely make sure the childcare center is a good one. Get references. Ask the neighbors. Ask the childcare center about what kind of things they teach. Ask them about the physical environment. Parents must ask lots of questions to make sure they are leaving their children in a place where they are safe and will learn good things.

Getting an education is a most basic thing in life, as I mentioned before, starting in the womb; and from birth, a child learns from the people around him. So, we need to make sure that he starts learning good things. And we have to be vigilant they continue learning good things to the end of their childhoods.

We also have to make sure that they do not drop out of school for a flimsy reason. Lots of time when the kids are not doing well in particular subject, they start thinking of leaving school, as they do not want to be the laughingstock among their peers. That should be a sign for the parents to be vigilant. Another reason a child might want to leave school is that they are being bullied at school. So, at all the levels, parent's interaction with their kids is very important. They need to watch the kid's performance closely.

When the kids have to change schools when they go to high school from middle school or junior high can be challenging for some kids. This is so because when they go to a different school, they can lose their old friends. For some kids making new friends at that time in their lives becomes a little difficult because of their shy nature.

Many kids need help in completing their projects. When they do not get help from their parents, they look somewhere else. If they do not get the right help when they need it, they can become lost and frustrated. This again can be a factor in their wanting to drop out.

Also, an education does not just finish at high school. We should make sure that the child starts focusing on their career as soon as they are in high school (if not before) and planning further education to achieve that goal. School counselors can help the child decide what he or she wants to do in life. Counselors are trained and have experience to guide the child in one of their favorite subjects and according to their aptitude.

It is important to start planning your child's college education when they enter high school so they can begin to plot the course of their future by choosing the right subjects to study. If money is an issue, there are lots of grants available for a college education to help you and your children financially. You can also make use of the internet and local library or ask the school administration about the grants and loans available for higher education for the kids.

Remember, it is a proud moment for the parents to see their child doing well in life.

# Chapter 3: Television & Video Games

Limit the amount of television they watch. Also, pay attention to what kind of programs they are watching and what video games they play. Have we given a thought to this as to why the kids are getting so aggressive and talk about guns nowadays? A lot of it comes from what they see and do. When a kid is playing a video game, he is picturing himself as a hero with a gun in his hand. To win, he has to kill all the people, characters, or creatures he comes across in the game. There is already anger building up in many kids for various reasons (broken families, abuse of drugs, economic differences, lack of knowledge, fights in the house, being ridiculed, and so, when he comes out of the game, he wants to do the same thing in real life too, i.e. to kill. Aren't we seeing this sad process come to fruition more and more over the past few years in the form of school and university killings? If we keep on going on the same track and do not do anything to make it better, unfortunately we may see more of this kind of carnage. And yet we rely on these electronic devices as virtual babysitters.

For example, often when some adults are talking and a kid comes and start talking, asking questions, distracting the adult, sometimes to get attention, the adult merely hands the child a cell phone or a video game to divert their attention. If you have ever done this, consider the results of this simple action. First of all, he may think that you do not want to give him your time; secondly, for him playing a video game anytime is now interpreted as being okay; thirdly, you are making him a video game addict, ruining his eye sight and health. He should be going outside and playing, but you encourage him to play video games only because he was distracting you from your conversation or work.

Child psychologist Dr. Stephanie Mihalas advises parents to keep track of the types of games their kids are playing and how much time they spend on them. Dr. Mihalas also says that there should be an open dialogue between the parents and kids. Parents should ask their kids upfront how they feel about killing people or creatures in the game. If you communicate with them, you will be conscious of their psychology, but moreover you will have the opportunity to emphasize that video games are just for fun and not real. The same strategy is applicable to the reality television shows.

Limiting exposure to video games is important too, however. Dr. Mihalas notes exposure to electronic media can affect the brains of certain children in a negative way. And Doctor Kaveri Subrahmanyam observes that media has short-term effects on a person as it desensitizes us to that which is around us. However, it also has long-term effects on kids who are already frustrated and have symptoms of a high degree of aggression. Effectively, when they consume violence and have problems with life, they are at risk of committing such acts. She further adds that reality shows that promote cruelty and social aggression further aggravate the tendency to violence for such individuals. The same goes with the reality shows that are full of sexual content.

A lack of sensitivity towards people combined with the media's persuasion creates aggression especially among people who are already aggressive. Moreover, 10-20% of individuals who are prone to violence may tend to get aggressive through media and video games.

Is your child so engrossed in video games that he is totally disconnected from the real world? It is not that playing video games is completely wrong. In fact, they have been shown to sharpen the mind, skills, and reflexes, and they also make kids more creative. Video games can help them in advanced critical thinking as they tackle various moves spontaneously in the games. However, this is all a moot point if some games make kids hyper, angry, and aggressive. The ratio of positive to negative effects also depends as to how much time they spend playing the video games. They can really get addicted to the video games, which can hinder their natural growth.

Juan Campos explains that kids are prone to sex, crime, and gang culture. Most of the media is about money, drugs, and women. And apparently, our media and game developers are promoting these same themes. Sadly, some kids think that this is what they want. They watch television and think whatever is being broadcast is cool.

However, playing video games can be likened to using drugs. I know there are millions of devoted gamers, a good portion of whom are adults! But the truth remains that video games can be just as addicting as any drug around. Look at a simple game like "Candy Crush." People get hooked to it. The point is this: Many young people are more than just interested in these games, which should clearly indicate that these so-called pastimes are like drug dependence for many.

As much as the video games make one's mind or reflexes sharper, they can also cause a host of medical and emotional problems, such as obesity, hypertension, loneliness, etc. When you play video games, your eyes do not blink naturally. Your eyes are supposed to blink 20 times in a minute, which is a nature's way to keep the eyes moist. Now, when they do not blink for so long, the eyes get dry and itchy. Then kids start rubbing them vigorously, which is going to affect their eyesight very fast. And repetitive motion of their hands may result in getting medical conditions like carpal tunnel, which is painful and has to be sometimes treated with surgery. Once that happens, the hands are not the same. Consider this: if they wish to be a doctor, nurse, architect, or even a handyman, their hands are not going to function in natural way once they have a problem like carpal tunnel.

When children play video games, they get so absorbed in it that they become a character un the game. They think that they are the heroes of the game, and they have to *Kill, Kill, and Kill*. These are completely negative vibes for the brain. These game-addicted kids also lose physical contact with friends, become aloof loners who then slowly become recluses and social outcasts. According to Vandana Kumar, their aloofness is also bringing a sense of lack of adjustment in today's children. They are having problems adjusting or getting along with their peers. They also then have an issue with conversation and communication with others. Juan Campos has observed that even kids sitting next to each other, instead of conversing, prefer to text each other.

Likewise, watching television is not bad in and of itself, but spending too much time watching it is definitely bad. Spending 30 minutes to an hour a day in front of the television is not considered bad. Watching unnecessary television is very unproductive, however. Children are wasting their time when they should be doing something creative or productive, like finishing their homework, working on a project, doing some hobby work, or playing outdoors.

Secondly, however, it is important to consider the type of programs a child watches as it can affect their psychology either positively or negatively. Television is a great source of entertainment and information. For example, channels like Discovery give lots of information. There is huge amount of research involved in the programs they produce and bring to us and children can get a lot of knowledge from those programs.

But there are also programs that contain lots of sex, drama, violence, and negativity. Those are even rated because they are not fit for a certain age group. However, when we are watching those programs, we do not care what the rating is or whether our kids are watching them too. For an example, say we are watching an R-rated movie or drama and our 12 year-old child is sitting next to us and also watching it. We get so engrossed in the movie or that drama that we do not even think that this movie/drama is not fit to be seen by a 12 year-old, for whom getting exposure too early in life to these topics or images can have a negative effect.

But how much of the time do we even know what channels our kids are watching? The human mind is curious. It wants to see and explore things, but it also has to be controlled so that it does not wander in wrong directions. So, children watching wrong or inappropriate channels or programs have to be checked because these inappropriate programs can completely change their character and life if they start watching too young.

For example, most soap operas are full of negative characterizations, sex, and violence. Children watching such programs try to emulate those things. But it should be noted that watching negativity can affect any person of any age group, not only children. Such images merely affect children more as their mind is not completely developed and they cannot analyze the wrong or the right of a given situation.

As I said earlier, the human mind is very inquisitive. It wants to know more about others. It wants to know more about what is happening in others' homes rather than concentrating on what is happening in our own house. That is one of the reason why people gossip. The television companies make the programs and soap operas based on the inquisitive human nature. Why do you think programs like "Kardashians" become so successful? It is only that, as humans, we have more interest peeping into others' lives than making our own lives better. These kinds of programs are poison for our subconscious minds and cash cows for the producers of the shows because people can easily get hooked to such programming.

The gossiping, bickering, and sex in those programs takes over an adult and sometimes eventually their children. Remember, the actors working in those programs are paid heavily, and it is their profession. For the production companies making these programs there is a big money coming in from these programs. That is why they purposely make them raunchy and juicy for them to sell. However, we fail to notice how these programs are also affecting the subliminal brain and the character of our children.

# Chapter 4: Outdoors

Excessive television watching and video game playing are also taking a toll on children's physical health. Exercise is good for the body, mind, and soul. It brings in a positive energy. Being outside in the sun to play makes the bones and body stronger. You get Vitamin D in natural form, which is crucial to build strong bones. It also brings more positives in the form of making friends and making those friendship bonds stronger. And yet we see fewer kids on the playgrounds now.

Think about the times when just rolling on the grass, doing simple stuff on the fields or park gave such immense pleasure to the mind. Do you remember what thrill it gave us when we used to roll down a hill, fly a kite, run after chickens or butterflies, or climb trees! I doubt most kids now even know about these simple and fun things in life.

Outdoor playing gives a child sense of freedom to do their own thing, to be just themselves, or with their friends. So, we must not let the kid in them die. And many kids have extra energy, and they do not know how to let it out. Parents should channel their energy in the right direction by putting them in some sport. If that energy is channeled in the right direction, your kid will get a direction and also that energy will not go in a negative direction.

Likewise, outdoor games give a positive attitude and a boost of energy to children. It makes the kids stronger inside and out, as it builds and boosts their immune system. Kids who play outside have relatively less stress. They are happier. It gives them more Vitamin D naturally through the sun, and makes their bones stronger.

As quoted in the report "Childhood and Nature: Natural England 2009," adults stated that they played outdoors for more than 40% of their time as kids but today kids spend only 10% of their time outdoors. Moreover, kids spend an average of 5 hours 30 minutes a day in front of television or a computer screen. And per the National Health Service (NHS), in 2009-10 28% of boys and 37% of girls were in the obese category while in primary school. Obesity is linked to health problems that lead to diabetes, heart disease, and cancer as kids grow up. More and more kids are becoming couch potatoes just because of lack of outside play. They are spending more time in front of television, computers, and video games. They do not even want to get up to get a glass of water or dinner, as they want to eat right there, in front of the television or computer. Is it any wonder so many are obese?

Another research study found that only a small percentage of kids use the parks mostly during summers, but only if it is sunny, and kids tend to avoid it altogether during the other seasons. This implies that kids have no access to outdoors during winter.

As per a University of Essex report from 2009, "Nature, Childhood, Health and Life Pathways," kids contact with the nature and physical activity not only affects their well-being but growth and long-term health. Moreover, playing outdoors has a positive effect on a kid's mental health. For instance, per Taylor et al in "Coping with ADD" (2001), the more natural activity a child engages in the less chance they have of developing attention deficit symptoms. Another research project indicates that time spent in green spaces relaxes the mind and helps children recover from stress and mental fatigue. It can also reduce aggression and has a calming and therapeutic effect.

A child's relationship with nature is also critical for them to learn about the natural environment. It helps kids understand how to care for nature. But when kids are outdoors, they not only learn about nature and wildlife. They get an opportunity to be loud and make noise; they are energetic and exuberant; they learn to be inquisitive and learn to explore their surroundings; they learn how to be creative and imaginative yet at the same time messy.

Remember, an idle mind is a mind that Satan can use. Controlling the mind is the most difficult thing in the world. So, when the mind does not have anything to do, it will start wandering in different or wrong directions. Indeed, most of the time it wanders in a negative direction.

Kids who spend more time inside the house in front of their computers and video games are found to be lonely, remorseful, cranky, stressful, obese, sick with more ailments (physical and mental) than compared to the kids who play more outdoors. Outdoor activities, like playing games such as soccer or basketball focuses the mind to a positive activity. It also brings in a sense of camaraderie and teaches them how to become a team player, which also can help later in their career.

Vandana Kumar mentioned that the kids often complain about boredom. This may be because there is no change in activity in their lives. For them a change in activity means switching from Facebook to YouTube or chatting. She suggests the importance of teaching kids the real change in activity, like switching from surfing on the internet to helping in the kitchen or doing laundry, or switching from watching TV to going outside to play. That change in activity in their lives will keep them healthy and creative.

Here are some quick tips to help you reconnect your child with nature:

- Make sure your child gets plenty of outdoor time all year round. Being in tune with the change of seasons will keep your child in sync with the rhythm of nature.

- When possible, visit beautiful natural settings, including local parks and gardens.

- For your next vacation, bypass the theme park and head to a national park.

- Watch the Discovery Channel with your child so he can partake of the wonder of nature on a regular basis.

- Encourage your child to play outdoor sports.

- Take the time to stop and notice the natural beauty that surrounds you and your child, whether it's in the middle of a large urban area or in the country.

Remember, it is up to you. If you want your kids to be healthier and stronger, push them out to play; and play with them as well.

# Chapter 5: Obesity/Health

Whereas past AMA documents have referred to obesity as an urgent chronic condition a major health concern and a complex disorder, on June 18, 2013, the American Medical Association declared that obesity is a disease that effectively defines 78 Million American adults and 12 million children as having a medical condition requiring treatment. The nation's leading physicians' organization took the vote after debating whether the action would do more to help affected patients get useful treatment or would further stigmatize a condition with many causes and few easy fixes. As per Dr. Patrice Harris an AMA board member, recognizing obesity as a disease will help change the way the medical community tackles this complex issue that affects approximately one in three Americans.

America has become a land of obesity thanks to the junk food culture and corporate greed. Corporations entice kids with colorful commercials to eat their sugary and fattening foods, and if you notice the changes happening in the kids' health in the last few decades; if you remember how the kids looked 30 years ago and how they look now, you will know that there is a connection between the corporate greed of food companies and Obesity.

The way that the food corporations describe their foods is so deceiving. Few people know that diet sodas, are actually more harmful than regular sodas or that fat-free products often contain added sugar and therefore calories.

In order to understand this epidemic, we first must understand what obesity is. If your child's weight is less than 10 percent above the recommended weight for his or her height and body type, the child is not considered obese, just a little overweight. However, if the child's weight is more than 10 percent over the recommended weight, the child is considered obese. And an obese child has a more than 80 percent chance of being obese when adult. And if one parent is obese, then the chance of their child becoming obese is about 40 to

50 percent. However, if both parents are obese, then the chances of the child becoming obese are much higher.

Obesity mainly happens due to a bad diet, bad eating habits, and a lack of physical exercise. It some cases, it may happen due to certain medical conditions or as a side effect of certain medications. However, that ratio of the obese is small.

The main causes of obesity are as follows:

- Eating junk foods, and intake of excessive sugars & sodas

- Overeating

- One of the parents being obese

- Lack of physical exercise or outdoor activities

- Being a couch potato (sitting in front of a TV or playing video games for long hours)

- Depression

- Stress

- Side effect of certain medications

- Medical problems

Obesity can lead to a host of other problems, like diabetes, hypertension, and heart failure. There can be psychological problems too.

As a parent, you can avoid obesity for your children by refusing to overfeed them and by not giving them junk food. It is fine to indulge once in a while in the junk foods, but most of their food habits should be healthy so that they become responsible eaters. Give them more green vegetables. Meats can give them protein, but nature has put an abundance of vitamins and minerals in vegetables. If your diet is right, lots of health complications vanish automatically. Hundreds of thousands people die every year in the USA due to problems related to obesity. In fact, per a recent study, 18% of obese people die due to obesity related problems. But worldwide more and more people are cutting down on meat, and some are turning to vegetarianism to stay healthier.

Pulmonologist Gurdip Flora, MD suggests that a lot of health related issues are linked to time. Kids are under a lot of pressure to perform and do their homework. Parents typically prefer giving quick meals to their busy kids, which doesn't provide them with proper nutrition. Moreover, parents find it difficult to commit quality time to their kids. Television time in combination with the pressure of homework leads to sleep deprivation in kids. The situation is further aggravated by sleep disorders in kids, which desensitizes kids to fast food.

As mentioned earlier, the food companies make their advertisements fascinating so that kids and adults will want their food products. They also have their products displayed in the store in such a way as to entice you to get it. Have you noticed that the food companies have all the candies placed next to the cashier in stores? We have all seen how this works. A mom is about to pay the cashier when her child places a pack of candies before the cashier and says he or she wants this. As soon as the mom says no, the tantrum starts. Most of the time, moms will give in and get the pack of candies for their kid even though it is nothing but sugar and extra calories going in her child's body. Apart from the extra (junk) calories, the sugar makes the child more hyper too.

Recently, I saw a video on YouTube.com about the ill effects of sugar. According to that video excessive sugar is harming the health of Americans so fast that more than 250 million Americans are suffering from issues like lupus and gastrointestinal disorders. Sugar has no nutritional value. In fact, it is addicting and toxic. Food companies are using different terms for refined sugars to sneak them past the discerning consumer who reads labels too, calling it agave nectar, dextrose, malt syrup, and so on. As I mentioned that sugar has no nutritional value. However, it definitely helps you to increase your weight and even to become obese.

In fact, everyone should check the ingredients of the items you pick up from the stores because ultimately you are responsible for the type of food you are giving your kids. Corporations mainly worry about their profits, but it is you who should be aware of what are you feeding your children.

If you check the sugar content for every product you purchase, you will be unpleasantly surprised to find out that literally each and every food item contains sugar. If on top of all the sugar in everyday food items we give children candies, chocolates, and more candies every day, it is no wonder they are getting obese.

Have you ever realized that the fast food companies are making the size of burgers smaller and sodas bigger? Have you wondered why? It is because they have much more profits in selling a soda. The soda companies want you to drink more sodas so that you get addicted to their brand. Moreover the sugar in it is itself addicting. Now, let us see as to what that soda, which is nothing but sugary water, is doing to your body.

Each 12 oz. can of soda contains anywhere from 33 to 39 grams of sugar, which is equivalent to about 8 to 10 cubes of sugar. Few of us would ever eat that much sugar in raw form at one time, and yet we give soda to our kids, and that can of soda is taking them closer to becoming diabetic and obese much faster. We haven't even talked about the effects the sodas have on the bones and the teeth. In certain sodas and drinks, an ingredient called BVO, or Brominated Vegetable Oil, is added to prevent the flavoring from separating from the drink. BVO is an industrial chemical used as a flame retardant in plastics. This chemical is known to cause memory loss and nerve disorders when consumed in large quantities. BVO is banned in Europe and Japan as a food additive. So, we are not just drinking a soda, but rather, it is a slow poison for our body.

Selling "combo" meals is another way food companies make their money and make you fat in the process. You are hungry, and the burger itself can fill you up. But you want to have a combo with all the fries and soda, and for just 75 cents more you can make your combo super-size. Do you really need to eat that much?

According to Doctor Flora, sodas have a further negative effect on our weight because they expand your stomach temporarily, so you tend to eat more than your requirement. So, instead of sodas, have your kids drink homemade lemonade. It is cheaper, refreshing, full of actual vitamin C, low in sugar, and moreover, there is Mom's love in it.

Or make a refreshing smoothie for your children. Get some fruits together, put them in a blender, add a little ice, and you have a delicious and nutritious smoothie. It takes just a few minutes, and once they get hooked on drinkable fruit, they will love you even more. It is much better getting hooked to this type of drink than sodas.

Better still; teach them how to make smoothies. There is a saying: "Give a man a fish and you feed him for a day. Teach a man to fish and you feed him for a lifetime." That is, once you teach your children how to provide healthy meals for themselves, there is a chance that the will last them a lifetime and that they may teach this to their kids too.

As much as possible, we should also avoid giving red meats to the kids. Studies show that red meat helps you to get protein, niacin, Vitamin B-12, iron, and zinc in your body. However, it is also medically proven that you get lots of saturated fat by eating red meat that can lead to clogged arteries, which can lead to heart complications. Studies have also shown that those who regularly ate a diet high in red meats, desserts, refined grains, and French fries had an increased risk of heart disease and cancer. Red meat also takes longer to get digested, which can be a cause of constipation. When you get constipated, you take extra medications for that condition and taking that extra medication may have side effects.

So, if we look at the benefits of eating red meat versus the negative effects, the negative effects outweigh the positive. The protein and vitamins red meat provides can be had from poultry, fish, vegetables, and pulses too. That way you don't have to worry about high cholesterol.

So, add more veggies in your kitchen. It will be much better for your kids and they will have a healthier future.

# Chapter 6: Science, Technology, & Electronics

Science, technology, and electronics have changed the world we live in, making work easier and bringing people closer together because of improved communication. They have also given us a way to entertain ourselves, even if we are alone. You can download music, movies, and soap operas and listen to or watch what you have downloaded at your own convenience.

As a result of improved technology, television and computers, the internet and smartphones, have become a part of every household. These electronic innovations help us and our children in many ways. They are educational and keep us informed. However, they can also influence the kids in a negative way. Kids can learn undesirable things from them.

Moreover, the time spent on watching television, being on the internet, or playing video games takes away time for important things such as playing outdoors, spending time with family, and etc. These technologies can make kids loners, also. Many children live more in a fantasy (virtual) world than in real world, and they cannot tell the difference between these fantasies from reality. For them a friend on the internet would be the same as a friend in real life, but they do not know who might be on the other end faking being their friend. It may be a pedophile waiting to strike.

Vandana Kumar, a well-established teacher, mentions that the internet is worse for kids than it is good for them. Kids end up watching videos that they should not be looking at. Moreover, kids end up clarifying their action with explanations such as, "This is the way things work today." They have no focus and concentration. Their hormones are raging. They do not know how to use games for education. Rather, the games today are filled with violence and sex.

Kids watching television also get influenced by exotic commercials, which the big corporations specially put on the kids channels. They know very well how to catch influence children. Have you noticed how they place commercials between and during kids' programs?

When the kids are really engrossed watching a particular program, and when that character or actor in the program is about to eat a cereal or breakfast, a commercial for some cereal company interrupts the program. The kid's subconscious connects the program and the fact they like it with the commercial and now the kid wants just that cereal, whether or not that particular cereal is healthy for him?

Another example: He is watching a program of an action hero. As the action hero is about to fly or hit the bad guy, right then they drop a commercial of an energy drink. Wow! That works for the company. Now, the kid is watching all that action, and the energy drink's commercial suggests having that drink to get all that incredible energy. What do you think the kid is going to ask you next? You guessed right: that energy drink. And if you don't get it for him, he may try other means to get it because he wants it now. Some parents may think, "What the heck. It's just an energy drink. Let us get it for him." But does your child need that energy drink in the first place, and do you even know what that energy drink contains? Do you realize that it is full of caffeine and other chemicals that can do more harm to your kid's body than good?

There are far more issues associated with children and media, and many are not what you might think. For example, a lot of adults love to watch porn. The cable companies know exactly what exactly you watch. In fact, they know your psyche almost better than you do, and they are in business to sell you the type of entertainment you want. Since they know you love watching porn, for example, they offer you such an incredible offer to subscribe to a package that you cannot refuse: a penny a month for the next three months. Well, you get it, and you start enjoying that package, but did you forget to put a Child Lock on those channels?

You would be surprised how many people forget this, and guess what? In your absence, your kid finds that channel; and do you think the kid is going to let it go? Human nature and curiosity have him taking a look, and thereafter the kid will start looking for a chance to watch that channel when you are not around. It does not seem necessary to delineate the negative influences happening in this situation.

Please do not get it wrong here. Watching television is not wrong, but you have to know what your kids are watching. And commercials on kids' channels are not such a big deal if you can make your children understand them. You need to educate them how the big corporations operate. You also need to tell them that it is not practical to buy everything they see on the television, but also that a given product may not be a healthy option. Like I mentioned in an earlier chapter, introduce them to healthy and informative channels, like Discovery, History, and National Geographic channels. It will also help them in their education.

In the last 20 years, electronic technology has developed by leaps and bounds. So television is not necessarily the biggest worry you face when it comes to your children and their interaction with technology. For example, social media has made the world much smaller. You can talk or virtually socialize with people across the globe. Social media has brought a cultural revolution because you can learn so many things by using it. People have found long lost friends and relatives through the social media. You can post your latest pictures and let your friends and relatives across the globe see them right away. You can advertise your business and exchange ideas with people you will never meet face to face. The options are endless. It is just amazing, what you can do with it.

But social media has also brought some evils with it. Facebook is phenomenal, but it also has a dark side to it. If you do not turn on the right features, your identity is everywhere. You, your pictures, and data become public. Anyone can access it. Someone can retrieve your picture, morph it, and put it back on the internet. There are many sick minds around us. People with a sadistic nature feel happy by making others miserable.

I came across a Facebook post about a teacher who was trying to show how fast your photos can be shared on the internet. I got interested in the post and started looking at the comments people made. I was pleasantly surprised that many people were saying that parents should be looking over their children's shoulders to see what they are posting on Facebook and the sites they are visiting on the internet. However, it was disgusting to see how people can change the whole message and even a nice picture of a family or an individual to look gross. It was evident from the way some people altered the picture of that teacher, who posted that feature. This also sends a message to everyone to post their pictures judiciously.

I am not criticizing the Facebook, as it has helped people connect and has done tremendously well with its other features. However, it has also created the wormholes for some sick-minded people to prey on innocent children and for certain sadists who alter people's pictures through Photoshop and repost them on the internet.

I would like to quote Mr. Campos here, who told me that quite a few kids just shoot each other's pictures (sometimes in inappropriate poses) with their smart phones and then get into trouble. Kids do not know what is in others' minds. Things done innocently can get them in trouble as the person taking that picture can either start blackmailing them or post the pictures on the internet. And many times the pictures get morphed before being posted online. So, it is important to educate your kids, not to let anyone take their inappropriate pictures even as fun.

Then there are people who prey on innocent children. Pedophiles are lurking everywhere on the internet, waiting for a chance to strike. They get into chat rooms, pretending to be teens, and mingle with the kids. These pedophiles befriend children, faking their true identity and pretending to be teenagers or young children. Then they ask children about their personal information such as to where do they live or go to school and for contact numbers so that they can prey on them, making these innocent children vulnerable. Lots of parents do not seem to care what their children are doing on the internet, and now it has become easier for kids to have internet access with the advent of smart phones and iPads.

The idea is to know where children are surfing on the internet, especially when they are in teens, as it is a very vulnerable age. That is the age when children think that they know it all and their parents do not. Facebook, as of Oct. 2013, has lifted restrictions on kids ages 13 to 17? Prior to that date, teens' posts on Facebook could be viewed only by friends and the friends of their friends. Now they are allowing kids 13 to 17 to share information with people they do not know. This can be scary!

Obviously, we parents need to educate ourselves first, and then we need to educate our kids about the ramifications of all these issues. If we do not know about the issues, how are we going to educate them about these issues? If we simply ask them not to do something in particular, they are not going to listen. However, they may listen if you give them a reason.

Larry D. Rosen, PhD, Professor of Psychology at California State University, Dominguez Hills, CA mentioned at the APA's 2011 Annual Convention that the children whose parents do not ask them about their online activities and do not monitor their use of Facebook are less healthy, more narcissistic, and perform worse at school than children whose parents restrict their technology use. In his research on how Facebook and other technologies affect the health and well-being of today's youth, Larry Rosen found that students who use Facebook throughout the day are prone to mental health problems, have worse grades, and tend to be sick compared to their peers, who use social media less frequently.

In another study, which was conducted in 2009, Rosen surveyed 1000 parents about how much time their kids spend online, their eating habits, exercise routine, overall physical and mental health, and their use of other technology, such as video gaming systems. Mr. Rosen found that even when he accounted for demographics, eating habits, and lack of exercise, media and technology still had a powerful effect on these children's health.

Those who used more hours of media were unhealthier across the board, from elementary school age through high school, said Rosen. They reported more sick days, more stomach aches, more depression, and worse behavior in school. You name it, they had more of it, he said.

To see whether social media had a similar effect on mental health, Rosen conducted a follow-up study this year to look at whether frequent use of social media, especially of Facebook, could predict signs and symptoms of personality disorders among young users. His preliminary findings show that frequent Facebook use among teens correlates only with narcissism, but for young adults, it correlates with signs of many disorders, including narcissism, antisocial personality disorder, bipolar disorder, and borderline personality disorder.

Despite such evidence, Rosen—who is a fan of Facebook himself—said he believes that there are positive aspects to social media use among youth. In 2011, he and colleagues found that young adults who spend more time on Facebook than their peers are also better at showing "virtual empathy" to their online friends and that such online empathy predicts real-world empathy.

"There even appears, statistically, to be a causal link there, that they are practicing it, putting the real-world empathy out there," said Rosen. "The more time they spend interacting, sharing and connecting online, the more real-world empathy they have."

The parenting style is what can make the difference between too much Facebook and just the right amount, added Rosen. In a 2008 study, he found that when parents use an authoritative style—establishing firm rules about online use, setting clear limits, and talking about possible negative consequences in advance—their children tend to use the Internet in moderation and have more self-esteem and less depression than peers with parents who aren't as rules-oriented.

"We can't simply assume that we can trust what [our children] are doing," he said. We also can't go the other way and attach software to their computers that monitors their keystrokes. Most kids could figure that out in five minutes."

Instead, parents should assess their child's activities on social networking sites, and discuss removing inappropriate content or connections to people who appear problematic. Parents also need to pay attention to the online trends and the latest technologies, websites and applications children are using, he said.

"You need to talk to your kids, or rather, listen to them," Rosen said. "Talk one minute and listen for five."

If your teens are not listening to you about their social media and internet activities, then let them know what General Martin Dempsey, Chairman of the Joint Chiefs of Staff, has to say in this regard. General Dempsey is a top General at the Pentagon.

As per Time's staff and wire reports of Los Angeles (Dec. 4, 2013), Dempsey, in his address at a Washington conference, indicated that the next generation of possible military recruits are ignorant about the damage that can come from showing bad or illegal behavior online. He mentioned that he worries about the young men and women who are now in their early teens who probably underestimate the impact of their persona in social media and what impact that could have later in life on things like security clearances and promotions.

In other words, teens are telling too much about themselves, their nature, and behavior to the whole world on social media, which may disqualify them from service or federal jobs. However, this warning also applies to people seeking private sector jobs, as the companies check the personal social media accounts of people who apply. Consequently, it is important for parents as well as teachers to help kids with their online persona so they not only avoid problems in the present but in their future lives as well.

Vandana Kumar adds to this argument by saying that many children are becoming loners. They are not emotionally interactive. They merely delete people if they do not like them, which has become a trend these days. Either they like someone or they hate them. There is no middle ground for them, which will become difficult for them when they have to share an apartment or a dorm room with someone during their college years.

The situation is obviously different for a kid raised amongst cousins and other relatives, who learns the sharing and caring concept automatically. That kid will also learn adjusting with others more easily. It is really difficult, in our times, when we have nuclear family concept, but we can try inculcating such values in our kids in their early lives anyway so that they do not suffer from an inability to compromise or interact with others when they grow up.

**Cell Phones/Texting:**

Researchers and commentators have termed the generations of the last several decades as Generation X, born from the mid-1960s through the 1970s, and Generation Y, also known as the Millennial Generation, born in the 1980s and 1990s.

People from the former generation are shown to be educated, active, balanced, and family-oriented; and people from the latter are more technology driven. However, they are also more aloof, lonely, and in-their-own-world. They are socially active on social sites, but when it comes to actual interaction with people, they don't get comfortable. They get nervous easily. They are also found to be impatient and expect instant gratification. They are the kids or youngsters whose best friend is either their smart phones or iPads. They have hundreds or even thousands of online (virtual) friends whom they have never met but very few, or in some cases, no actual friends.

What surprises me is that even some of school districts are insisting on getting iPads for the kids as young as four years old. There is no research involved as to why and how it is going to benefit the kids if they are introduced to the iPads at that early age, and the schools also do not know how the kids are going to use those iPads. They just want to introduce the technology. The Los Angles United School District (LAUSD), for an instance, has been criticized lately because, without any research or planning, they wanted to give IPads the students, and at an exorbitant cost of $900 per iPad.

But a bigger issue more broadly used has to do with cell phones and texting now. On May 13, 2013 someone shared a video on Facebook that was really sad. A beautiful girl (in her early 20s) was announced to have breast cancer. In the FB video, a cancer specialist, Doctor Randall Oyer, mentions that it is not the age to get a breast cancer, but a common habit of teenage girls may have led to the cancer this young woman got. She was in a habit of putting her cell phone next to her breast, tucked in her bra. In fact, the cancer started right at that point, where she used to keep the cell phone. Doctor Randall also mentioned that he had another similar case earlier.

There was a news item in a Los Angeles newspaper regarding where people keep their smart phones. It said that it is so clear that people are hooked to their smart phones because, in a survey, nearly three in four smart phone users in the U.S. said that they are within five feet of their devices most of the time. Surprisingly, many of the users said they use their smart phones even in the shower. The funnier and the unusual fact is that many admitted using the smart phone while having sex. Have you noticed people using their smart phones during dinner or places of worship? The most disturbing is when they are at a funeral and the phone starts ringing.

Kids use their phones everywhere. They use smart phones while driving, cycling, even when they are riding a motorcycle. They get oblivious to the fact that they can get into an accident, which can hurt or kill them or someone else. How many accidents have we seen because some teenager was texting while driving? Texting while driving is being considered even worse than drunk driving as a public health hazard. But teens, and many adults, still text while driving in spite of such stories because it has become a habit for them, like an addiction.

Having their cell phones in easy reach all the time has other deleterious effects too. Have you noticed that today's children have a very short span of attention? You have to tell them everything twice before they understand it. They also complain of being tired as soon as they get up in the morning. To help rid themselves of that tiredness, they use synthetic drinks like Red Bull or Monster, which are full of sugar and caffeine.

But the cause is easy to discern. They are paying more attention to the phone than to you when you speak. In the night instead of taking a good night sleep, they are waiting for the next text from one of their friends (who is also apparently awake or half-asleep). So, when that text comes, the kid has to get up and check the text, and definitely reply to it. Even if it is just LOL (laugh out loud).

What is happening here is that the kid is not sleeping the way he should because his sub-conscious mind is awake. People need to go into deep sleep for complete relaxation of the body. It is nature's way to relax the body. With complete relaxation during deep sleep, the body also repairs itself. When that does not happen (as in this case, where the sub-conscious mind is awake), the child does not get complete rest and wakes up feeling tired. This keeps on happening every night and results in sleep deprivation.

Dr. Flora (an expert in sleep disorders) mentions that your body needs proper sleep. Because of our circadian rhythm, the body temperature drops twice a day, once around 2 pm and then between

10 and 11 pm. If the kid does not go to bed on time at night, and if his sleep is disturbed when they do, then they are susceptible to falling asleep around 2 pm. In order to stay awake in the class or for studies, they resort to drinking caffeine.

He further explains that the right amount and quality of sleep are also very important for the body to repair itself from everyday wear and tear. When people have their cell phones next to them, even on vibrate mode, it disturbs the sleep pattern. Sleep follows the pattern of non-REM and then REM sleep. We have three periods (N1, N2 and N3) of non-REM sleep, each period of non-REM sleep lasting from 90 to 120 minutes, which leads to REM sleep (which is also called deep sleep). N3 of non-REM sleep is where the body gets most of its repair from the daily wear and tear the body suffers due to walking, athletic activities, stress, and etc. The body needs four of those cycles, and if the sleep pattern (these cycles) gets disturbed in between, for example you get awakened because of your cell phone, these cycles have to start all over again from N1. The result is sleep deprivation and all the issues related to it.

So, the rule should be that, when the kids go to sleep, their phones should be either switched off or away from them. But not just lack of sleep is an issue born of this new technology.

Headline in *The L.A. Times*, Aug. 2013: "Texting on Your Feet can be a Safety Hazard." The report indicates that the Department of Transportation announced steps to combat the recent rise in pedestrian accidents partially due to what Secretary Anthony Fox called distracted walking.

Walking while texting, listening to music, or on drugs may have contributed to the increase in pedestrian accidents, Fox said, because being thus distracted impacts their ability to keep people safe. In the three cities with the highest percentage of pedestrian deaths relative to all traffic, 51% of all motor vehicle deaths in New York were pedestrians, 42% in Los Angeles, and 30% in Chicago. Further, more than 1500 pedestrians were treated in emergency rooms in 2011 after being injured while using portable electronic devices such as a cell phone, according to a recent US Consumer Products Safety

Commission report. Fox said that the answer was more enforcement and education, such as the pedestrian safety campaign.

Obviously, if used in a safe way and constructively, texting is a great tool for the kids, such as to help them with their studies as it can help them quickly exchange notes or ideas or get answers from their peers. Dr. Mihalas also suggests it fosters social interaction for kids. They learn from texting and it so makes sense for parents to encourage it subject to some moderation. Parents should set boundaries and should take away phones from their kids at night so that they are not distracted and can sleep well. An irony is that a lot of parents indulge themselves in texting at night. You cannot preach what you do not practice. Therefore, it is imperative for parents to first correct themselves and set the right example in front of their kids. Else, the parents will be seen as hypocritical.

However, a contrary position is worth considering. Vandana Kumar mentions that text messages are not a real means to communicate. Kids have stopped talking today. They don't even listen to their parents when they are texting. According to Kumar, kids used to GPS on their mobile have also lost all sense of direction and technology in general is becoming more of a bane than a boon. You will never be able to control your child's use of these technologies, of course, for they are a fact of life now; but these assertions are something to consider as you ponder how to have as much input as possible in their choices.

And speaking of amazing technology, consider how music is delivered now, especially iPods. These things are amazing. There was a time when you would listen to 10 or 15 songs on a CD, and then you have to change the CD. Currently thousands of songs are available to you in a small portable device. You switch on your iPod, plug in those ear phones, and *wow*. You are listening to your favorite music, song after song. Everyone loves it, and your kids love it more than you. It's their thing. They love to have their earphones on all the time. They are in their own world.

But have you ever considered how many decibels of sound those earphones are throwing in their ears? Most portable music systems produce sound in the range of 95-108 decibels at level four and in excess of 115 Decibels at level eight.

Sound at 85 decibels or below is considered safe. For the sake of comparison: a soft whisper is usually measured at 30 decibels, a subway train at 90 decibels, a gunshot blast at 100 decibels, and a jet plane at 140 decibels.

Sounds above 140 Decibels usually cause pain. Have you seen people working on the airport tarmac wearing those earplugs? They may look funny, but they are protecting their ears from the constant high pitch sounds coming from aircraft. If they do not wear those earplugs, they can have severe hearing loss very quickly.

Have you ever considered that the constant use of loud music would eventually make your kids have a severe hearing loss or may even make them deaf at a very early age? You may have started this recently, but your kids probably started when they were 5, 6, or 7 years of age. Did you ever imagine that, even before you become grandparents, your own kid, who today may be in their twenties or thirties, could be experiencing hearing loss?

But then why would we even think about such consequences when we are doing it ourselves? For example, most gyms have loud music playing to encourage people to work out, but most of the people in the gym are still listening to their own music with their earplugs on. They are working on their body, which is good, but slowly and surely ruining their eardrums at the same time. Again, we need to get educated about these things first, and then educate our kids.

Now let's take a moment to think about the music kids are listening to. Two or three decades back, the music was mostly about love, caring, pain, and the sorrow of separation. The music of the current generation is all about drugs, killing, perverted sex, and so on.

Music is life, and music changes a person, and so we can only ponder the serious nature of the damage being done to children's psyches by listening to such lyrics. We know that music and lyrics can have a tremendous effect on your mood and subsequent behavior. For example, when the holiday season arrives, wherever you go you get to listen to Christmas jingles, which puts you in the mood of the holiday season. Likewise, when you listen to soothing music, your body feels relaxed; and when you listen to rock music, you start tapping your feet. In olden times, during the times of war they used to play loud patriotic music to get the people energized so that they get ready to fight.

So how can we possibly imagine that music that teaches the wrong things would not affect our children? In truth, such music can be pretty damaging to the personalities of the members of our young generation. It makes their mind perverted. All it teaches is to be "ghetto," that it is alright to use and abuse alcohol and drugs and to have sex with anyone. Where is it taking our kids? Kids get influenced very easily with these things. Many kids live in a fantasy land, and when they hear these things they take them to be a reality, and then want to follow what they hear.

Apart from changing their psyche with this kind of music and hearing loss, in perhaps 10 years we are going to see lots of kids who are teenagers today suffering from lots of different ailments very early in life. Have you wondered why?

It will be partly because of us.

Yes, us.

This is because, we are not stopping them to play video games non-stop.

This is because, they cannot even think of living without their cell phones.

This is because; they keep on texting each other, without any good reason.

Have you ever wondered what they text to each other about? Most of the time, it is just LOL or LMAO. They have their phones right next to them, even when they are sleeping, as discussed above. They want to reply to that text message they receive, right then and there. But their lack of sleep or distractedness is not the worst thing they face. Unfortunately, kids now days are living in their own "virtual world," and the larger ramifications of this for the kids and for our society have yet to be realized.

Also as discussed previously, and as Dr. Flora explains, one develops social skills from face-to face interaction, which is absent when you are depending too much on texting or excessive media use. This can lead to anti-social behavior, loneliness, and depression, which leads to adjustment issues when such a person must deal with others, including with co-workers or people in general at a later stage in life.

Dr. Flora further explains that continuous texting also hinders their ability to concentrate on a particular subject. For example if the kids are doing homework or studying while getting continuously distracted by texting or with social media, they cannot concentrate on their studies.

But far more than this, and far more simple is, being lost. Do you remember the days of getting together with your friends and laughing loudly at their jokes? In today's world, the kids laugh at their friends' jokes in a virtual manner, by just texting LOL or LMAO. There is no actual laughter, which is vanishing.

Laughter and crying are part of human nature, and if we take them out of our life, it is going to affect us in a negative way. This is making children more secluded, which in turn is slowly bringing stress and loneliness in their life—and unfortunately they do not realize it.

Lastly, I would like to make a point that discussing the same things a few times is important, as it reinforces the importance of the issue and embeds into the brain.

# Chapter 7: Friends

We make lot of friends in life. Some friends are good influence in our life; some do not influence us in any way; and some can be negative influence in our life. As adults, we can look back and figure out which friends influenced us in what way, but at that time, it was hard to figure out.

It can be the same situation for our kids too. Many kids are naïve and are not street savvy. They see every person in life the same way. They cannot see through people and are unable to make a sound judgment as to whether the person/friend is a good influence or a negative one. Sometimes it is too late, and by the time they figure that out, the damage is done.

So, it becomes very important that parents should know with whom their children are associating. Whereas, positive friends can help make a strong personality and help children to become a better person, associating with the wrong persons can ruin their life.

I always give my kids my own example in this regard. I was a reasonably good student until middle school. I had a friend who apparently got associated with the wrong people. One day after the physical training class, I was feeling little tired. My friend gave me half a pill and told me that it will kill the fatigue. Well, that was my first introduction to drugs.

Then, with couple of friends, I also started bunking classes. At that time, it felt like fun, but unfortunately, I started falling behind in my studies and then I failed in class. The result was that I lost one year of studies.

I tried that drug, which used to be called Mandrax, a couple of times. I was almost got hooked on them, but thank God and fortunately for me, my dad's transfer orders came right at that time and we had to move to a different city. It was a complete blessing for me and my family. After going to another city, I realized my mistake and shortcomings. I got back to my studies and ultimately completed my college degree.

Later on, I heard that my friend also moved to a different city and got serious about his life. So, for both of us, an unexpected move to another city may have come as a blessing in disguise and saved us. However, most people are not so fortunate. Once they take that route, they start falling into that black hole, and there is no end to that black hole. Unfortunately, their family suffers more than they do emotionally and, in most cases, economically too as they have to support the family and the victim's family too.

Many kids now expose themselves to the wrong people by talking to them openly on the Internet, where they do not even know the people they meet this way. They discuss their personal and family affairs with these people and become vulnerable to them. The next thing they know that pedophile is outside their house looking to lure them away. This can happen when you do not have a good communication with your child. He is looking for someone to talk to, and at vulnerable moments like this, they can be taken advantage of.

Know your children. Interact with them more. Just as parents should be speaking to their kids on an everyday basis about their school issues, problems, projects, and so on; parents also have a duty to know who their children's friends are. It is also important to know the family of their friends.

A few years back, one day, I went to see a friend. I noticed that he looked stressed and upset. I asked him if everything was fine. He answered in the negative. On asking him if I could be of any help, he took me to his office. I noticed that he was on the verge of crying. He told me that he found out that his only son was on drugs. He got to know that he had just started taking them. One of his son's friends got him into that. I asked him as to how much he interacts with his son on day-to-day basis. He told me that as he is always so busy with his business that he hardly gets time to talk to his son or family. I suggested him few things, like start going home early to be with his family. I also suggested that he should not get upset or yell at his son, that he should speak to him nicely instead of confronting him in an aggressive way, and that he should counsel him. He told me that he was taking his son to a counselor the next day. When I saw him a few days later, he looked relaxed and there was a smile on his face. After thanking me, he told me he was spending more time with his family and his son had understood the issue and promised not to see that friend any more, and that he is going to refrain from drugs.

Fortunately, in this case too there was an early detection of the problem, and it could be solved right away by taking some positive steps. The young boy was still in the experimenting stage and was not hooked on drugs.

This is one of the many reasons it is imperative to teach them from an early age to have good friends in life. Teach them to be associated with good people and not the wrong kind of people or friends who will take them to the path of destruction. As Warren Buffet says, "It is better to hang out with people better than you. Pick out associates whose behavior is better than yours and you will drift in that direction" The same holds for your kids.

Dr. Mihalas suggests that not only should parents know who their kids' friends are but where their kids are going; how long they will be gone, and who they are going with. It should be noted that openness requires years of trust and communication between parents and kids, which is a key for a strong relationship. Such nurturing should start when kids are small. Otherwise, when parents all of a sudden start setting boundaries for their kids when they are teens, their children will not listen.

# Chapter 8: Child Sex Abuse

Our society is full of a mix of people – good and bad. Some people would see children as innocent and lovable, but unfortunately, some see them as sex objects. Sexual abuse of children is becoming a virus in our society. Indeed, and unfortunately, it is a worldwide phenomenon.

One of our failures in regard to this terrible epidemic as parents is, to not to educate kids at the right time so that they do not become targets of such heinous people. Another issue, yet once again, is lack of effective communication between the parents and children.

We need to educate our children about the possibility of being approached by a pedophile as early as four or five years old. This is when they start learning about touching and understanding things a little bit, as they are preparing to go to school.

Lots of the information on the subject of child abuse for this book is from the website of the American Psychological Association (APA) at www.apa.org (with their consent and to educate the parents). I am thankful to them for letting me share this information.

Well, let us look at this issue of child abuse and understand what constitutes child sexual abuse: Child sexual abuse is any interaction between a child and an adult (or another child) in which the child is used for the sexual stimulation of the perpetrator or an observer. Children, due to their age and lack of knowledge about sex, cannot give meaningful consent to sexual activity.

Abuse to the child can be through deception, coercion, or force and may include touching or non-touching behaviors, which can include:

- Sexual kissing

- Inappropriate touching or fondling of the child's genitals, breasts, or buttocks

- Masturbation

- Oral-genital contact
- Oral or digital contact
- Forcing or enticing the child to watch pornography
- Exposing or flashing of one's body parts to the child
- Voyeurism (ogling of the child's body)
- Verbal pressure for sex

It is important to understand that children of any age, race, ethnicity, economic background, or culture can become a target of child sexual abuse, and that it does not matter if the child is a male or female.

It is also important to know that most abusers are people we are close to, people we know and trust such as family friends, a babysitter, neighbor, etc. However, an abuser could be a stranger, too. Now there are cases coming up where the educators and people from holy places have committed those crimes as well.

The APA lists some of the causes and risks as follows:

- Multiple caretakers of the child
- Caretaker or parent who has multiple sexual partners
- Drugs and alcohol abuse
- Poverty and living in poor neighborhoods
- Vulnerable child or child with lower self-esteem
- Poor supervision by the parents

The APA lists the following warning signs that sexual abuse has occurred:

- An increase in nightmares
- Angry outbursts
- Anxiety
- Depression
- Continual bed-wetting
- Difficulty in walking or sitting

- Loneliness or withdrawal behavior

- Pregnancy or venereal disease.

- Suicidal behavior

- Being secretive

- Reluctance to be left alone with a particular person or relative

A parent should take any changed behavior in their child as a potential sign, and take it very seriously. Do not scold your child because, in that case, the child will be more scared and may go into a shell. He may not discuss it with you the next time.

## Teach your children

You should teach your children basic sex education – a health professional can provide basic sexual education to your children if you feel uncomfortable doing so. Especially educate your kids at an appropriate age that any sexual advances from adults are wrong and teach them to let you know if anyone touches them in an inappropriate way, whether it is a stranger, a teacher, or any relative. Teach them the difference between "okay" and "not okay" touches, and educate them the accurate names for their private parts and how to take care of them (i.e., bathing, wiping after bathroom use) so they don't have to rely on adults or older children for help.

It is important that your children know they can make decisions about their own bodies and say "no" when they do not want to be touched or do not want to touch others (even refusing to give hugs). And make sure that you know your child's friends and their families. If you feel uneasy about leaving your child with someone, don't do it.

Let them know that, if they think someone is trying to touch them in wrong way, they should get away from that person right away, even if that person is an authority figure like a teacher or caretaker. And if there is still an issue, they should scream to get the attention of others.

## What you should do as a parent if you suspect abuse?

Give the child a safe environment in which to talk to you about the issue, and do not get angry or display unnecessary emotions. The child might go into defensive mode. Instead, stay calm and listen to what the child has to say before forming any conclusions.

Reassure the child that he or she has not done anything wrong. If you cannot handle the situation yourself, then get professional help from a psychologist or a mental health provider. Arrange for a medical examination of the child.

Many states require that individuals who know or suspect that a child has been sexually abused must report the abuse to local law enforcement or child protection officials. In all 50 states in the US, medical personnel, mental health professionals, teachers, and law enforcement personnel are required by law to report suspected abuse.

Here is some contact information for help in these kinds of situation. However, you may not have this information handy if and when something like this happens. Remember, the internet is a very powerful tool to find information at any given time.

And definitely ask for help. There are a number of organizations focused on assisting families dealing with child abuse:

- American Professional Society on the Abuse of Children www.apsac.org

- National Center for Missing and Exploited Children 24 hour hotline: 1-800-THE-LOST www.missingkids.com

- Child Help USA(1-800) 4-A-CHILD www.childhelp.org

- Prevent Child Abuse America (1-800) CHILDREN www.preventchildabuse.org

- Child Welfare Information Gateway (formerly National Clearinghouse on Child Abuse and Neglect Information) (1-800) 394-3366 www.childwelfare.gov

# Chapter 9: Helping Others

I mentioned earlier that, although she was not educated, my mother was smart and a good administrator. She started teaching us about the importance of helping others at the tender age of five or six, and it is in fact important to start teaching children about this topic early or they will not be as likely to understand the lesson. At night, when we all finished dinner, she would ask us to pick up our dishes. Once we learned that portion, that we are supposed to pick up our own dishes, the next step and instruction was that one of us has to pick up Dad's dishes too, as he has come from work tired.

Sometimes, she would take us for grocery shopping, so that we could help her carry the grocery bags. She also taught us to help her in the kitchen. She taught us to make basic dishes, like eggs and tea, with a dual purpose in mind. She wanted us to learn the importance of helping but she was teaching us to be independent too. This was that, in case of emergency, we could cook these basic dishes and not be hungry. We realized that latter part of her purpose later, when I was about 10 years old. My mom had to be hospitalized for two weeks due to some ailment, and during that time all the siblings would cook for the family, taking turns.

She taught us at an early age to help the old and needy without being asked. When travelling by bus, we were supposed to vacate the seat for the elderly or sick. Even when walking on the street, if we saw an older person carrying something heavy, my mom would tell us to ask the person if they would like our help.

I understand that the things are different than they were few decades back. You have to be a little cautious about other people. However, there are some basic courtesies in life, and if not imparted to our kids, they may not ever understand that fact.

Have you noticed that there is a change in how many kids behave compared to how the baby boomers behaved when we were kids? We would run to open the door for older people, and we loved helping them carry their groceries to their car. But this sight is rare today.

It is not the children's fault, however. It is our mistake that we are not teaching them what our parents or grandparents taught us. We are failing to teach them humility and empathy and to be good to our fellow human beings.

We can start by teaching them small things, like asking them to help in the kitchen. They can help you wash dishes, for example. They can also help you with the laundry so they learn how to do their own. This way they will not be dependent on you for such small things. They will also learn the importance of helping. Moreover, it will be family time together. Imagine how much fun it is talking to each other and doing things together. You can have the older siblings babysit for the younger siblings while you're away too. You are not only forming a habit within them to help but making your life easier too.

I was talking to my neighbor, who was complaining that her teenage son never offers to help her at fast food restaurant. She was upset that she toils the whole day six days a week, and unfortunately, her teenage son does not get it. Interestingly, she mentioned as to how she used to help her mother in her restaurant when she was in school.

At this, I told her that it may be her own fault. This is how our conversation went:

"So, Angela, did your mother ask you to help her in her restaurant after you got back from school?"

"Yes."

"Did you say no to her?"

"No, never."

"Did you like helping your mom?"

"Yes."

"Did your mom ask you to help her in your free time?"

"Yes."

"Did your mom make you realize how tired she gets with all that work and that she needed your help?"

"Yes, kind of."

"Did your mom teach you all about the restaurant and what to take care of?"

"She taught me the basics first and then everything else, and I loved it. And when there was no work, she would help me with my homework."

"Did you follow what your mom used to do? She just used to ask for help.

"Oh my God. I think you are right. I never asked my son to help me.

"Angela, that is your answer. It is that simple. We need to teach our kids, each and every day. Teaching them to be good adults comes from everyday real life experiences, which amounts to continuous education. We need to ask and educate, which we don't, and then later on, we complain. Then, when we complain, the kids do not understand what the issue is. They wonder why they are getting blamed. In your case, you never asked him to help and so you never taught your son to help you. So, how is he going to understand the meaning of help? Even if he knows about it, in general, we humans are lethargic by nature. We do not want to do anything extra, if we do not have to do it, and so he might need some prodding."

The crux of my conversation with Angela is that, if you do not teach your kids these basic things, they will not know the meaning of help; and further, then they will not teach these things to their kids. Eventually these small and very important courtesies of life will vanish if we do not teach our children in this way. The result in the coming years will be that we will create a mean and self-centered society. Would you want to give your kids that kind of legacy?

# Chapter 10: Counseling

Regularly counseling your children is the key to helping them to be good human beings. Counsel them every now and then about the good and bad things in life. Talk to them about different issues in their life. Sometimes, once is enough; but at other times, you may have to say the same thing again and again for them to remember it for lifetime. As I mentioned in an earlier chapter, telling our children the same thing a few times is important as it reinforces the importance of the issue, and the lesson also then embeds into their brain. You will notice that sometimes when you tell them something, they will just say okay but you know they are not even listening.

Obviously, your children can use your experience and guidance, but if you cannot guide them, get the help of someone you know who can do that for you in a positive way.

My wife and I had made it a point to counsel our children from an early age. When we picked them up or were dropping them off at school, on the way we used to discuss different things with them. We would ask them about school, their studies, their teachers, their classmates, etc. In a very cordial way we would ask them whether anyone had bullied them or if there was something they did not like about school. We would also take this chance, as we were driving to school or home, to talk to them about drugs, teen sex, or some other important subject. We would take that moment to talk to them about importance of ethics, education, career, being a good citizen, and etc. We would also talk about associating only with good people.

However, we made sure that we didn't overdo it, and our talks were never in the form of a lecture. Children hate being lectured, and so we always made it sort of a discussion, inviting their views and input. In fact, we noticed that once in a while, if we forgot to talk about something, our kids would start a conversation on the subject, which told us that they loved these talks as they were interested in learning those things. We never imposed anything on them. We just counseled and guided them in the right direction, in a very subtle way.

A child's brain is like fresh soil. Whatever seed you put in their brain, that seed will grow. If you plant a negative thorny bush, the outcome will be negative too. If you plant the right seed, beautiful flowers will blossom in the years to come. Remember, you are their first teachers, guides, and mentors. If you make a mistake, that mistake may come back to haunt you in the shape of your children's failures in life.

Dr. Mihalas emphasizes the importance of communication because it fosters trust between parents and kids. However, some parents think that they are being good parents by being friends to their children. And because of lack of supervision, they are often caught unaware by what goes on behind the scene. So just being friends with your children is not enough. You need to put proper supervision in place too.

We started to see the results of all our counseling as our kids grew older. By God's grace, and thanks to the right counseling, both our kids now have finished college. As this book is published, our older son graduated from UCLA with a degree in Economics and is completing his MBA. He is working full time in a good organization and studying part time for his Masters. The younger son completed his undergrad program majoring in Psychology from UC Riverside at the age of 20, two years ahead of schedule and is now helping us in business. Thanks to the Almighty, both our kids are educated, intelligent, humble, caring, and good to others. We can proudly say that they are good human beings.

However, in today's world, it can become difficult for parents to fulfill this role of counselor due to the stress in their professional and personal lives. Dr. Mihalas mentions that kids need a strong mentor in their life. It should be someone they trust, such as, their father, mother, or grandparents for this is critical for the development of a kid. But if the parents or grandparents are not able to perform this role, it is important to find the right mentor.

# Chapter 11: Quality Time

I read this quotation somewhere: Spending time with children is more important than spending money on children. It is important to remember that they not only need your guidance but want your company.

Do you remember the time of your childhood, when you would wait for your parents to come home, and as soon as they came through the door you would jump on them or reach up to them to get a hug. In the same way, have you noticed how your children get excited to see Mom or Dad come back from work? They want to converse with you. They want to tell you what happened in school today. They want to share their day's work with you. They want to tell you about their teacher. They may want to tell you that someone has bullied them at school. They want to ask you things. They want your help with their project. There are so many things in their plate.

But when you just tell them, "Hey, I am tired. Don't bug me right now." They get disheartened. They see that you just open your bottle of beer and lay on your couch watching television, and they don't know where to go or whom to ask. They feel helpless and dejected.

Today life is not easy and we all have a lot of stress. It may be job related stress, financial stress, relationship stress, or any other stress; and stress makes parenting very difficult, as you are coping with your own issues in life. However, it is not your children's fault, so why should they suffer because their parents cannot sit and talk to them.

The stress of life and of parenting itself is especially high for a single parent. Single parenting is itself a big job. However, it is essential to allow time for your children. In fact, you will see that, when you are with them and interacting with them positively, your stress level goes down. Perhaps you will find that you even forget about your issues and problems when you are interacting positively with your children.

When you are really stressed, try this: As soon as you get home, call your children and give them a nice hug and a few kisses. Then notice how your stress level goes down. This is called a Magical Hug, and it is a big stress reliever for you and gives immense happiness to your children.

It is completely understandable that, at times, you just want to be alone without any disturbance. At that moment, let your kids know that you want to be alone for some time and will speak to them little later. Do not yell at them. Let them know in a nice way. However, you may have to use your firm voice for this. If in a two-parent household, let your spouse handle the kids at that time. Most of the times kids will understand, but make sure you keep your promise to give them some time. Otherwise they will feel disheartened and cheated.

There are many positive things you can do with your kids. For example, kids love stories. You can educate them by telling them good stories as many have meaning or a message. This way you are spending time with them and also educating them in a subliminal way. They will remember those stories forever, along with the subtle messages.

You can also take them for a treat, which does not have to be expensive. Kids not only love treats but especially when it comes as a surprise. Moreover they love the family time together.

You can take them to the park and play outdoor games or even barbeque some food. Ask the kids to lend you a helping hand by marinating stuff or by serving everyone. Likewise you can take them camping or to the swimming pool, but if you are at home and do not want to go anywhere because you are tired, you can play board games with them.

Studies show that kids whose parents spend more quality time with them tend to do better in the school, and are more prone to be away from drugs. Just spending some quality time with your kids, talking to them about their work in school or asking them the progress in studies or about their projects, can help them grow and mature greatly. It also helps them bond with their family.

# Chapter 12: Listening

Communication between parents and children is very important. In fact, your kids always want to talk to you, so listen to them for they may have issues they want to talk to you about. Kids are also very innovative and may just want to share their great ideas and thoughts. Do not ignore them in the process or they may stop being innovative as they will discouraged. Overall, positive two-way communication builds their self-esteem and character.

A child who constantly interrupts adult conversation may be feeling starved for attention, and if you do not recognize and address this issue early, it slowly turns into a habit, which then starts irritating you. When your children were born, you constantly talked to them. You gave them so many hugs and kisses and talked about silly things with them. You didn't even care if the kid understood or not. You just loved it when your child responded with a laugh. However, as time passed and as the child grew, slowly you started losing your joy at their responses. Now you start getting irritated when the child asks you something. That may be because you had a long day at work or you did not have a good day. You may be irritated because you had an argument with your boss or a coworker, but your child does not know about that. So, when his dad or mom has come home, and he is seeing them after 8 to 10 hours, he is excited to touch you, hug you, or just talk to you. He may have stories to tell you about what happened at school, maybe that he got an "A" in a subject and the teacher praised him in front of the whole class; or he may be trying to tell you about some issue that is disturbing him. Then, when you do not have time to listen to him, he feels dejected or unimportant. He does not know where to go next. Now that child merely wants to let it out to someone. And so he interrupts you when you are on the phone or speaking to your spouse or just want some peace and quiet. He just needs to tell somebody.

Unfortunately, if you then send them away, they may find someone unsavory to share their news with instead of sharing it with a parent.

In fact, as noted previously, the internet and social media, which are great tools mostly, have also become tools to be used by people looking for these kinds of kids, who are either bored or have no one to talk to. They prey on these vulnerable kids. If you don't have time to listen to your kids, some "sicko" may have all the time necessary. He is just waiting for the opportunity.

Personally, I saw a post on the Facebook from a child saying he was bored at home alone and he had posted his telephone number for someone to call him. What do you think can happen in such instances?

On around August 1, 2013 there was news about the FBI rescuing 105 teenage kids from a child prostitution ring. In the news item, they mentioned that most of those kids were runaways from home, as they did not have a family bonding with their parents. It mentioned that the pimps lure these kinds of kids by becoming their friends or guardians etc. and then they exploit them.

It gets very difficult for the working parents to spend time with their kids, but why do we work so hard? It is so that we can give a good life to our family, and it is equally important to give them quality time. They just don't want only the toys and material things. They want you as well. In fact, they want more of you than they do toys. Sometimes we are surprised at the way kids come up with stories and at the things they say. They can be really funny at times and serious in their talk at other times. It is fun talking to them or just listening to them.

Remember, once time is gone, it does not come back. Once they grow up and have families of their own, you just cannot visit the old times. They will be just memories. So, why not create better memories for tomorrow by spending more time with them now. You will cherish those memories when you are sitting alone or with your family later in life. Those beautiful memories are pure gold.

# Chapter 13: Appreciation

Everyone likes to be appreciated by their boss, partner, spouse, and so on if they come up with some great idea or do something good. Kids are the same way. Show them appreciation for the nice things they do and see how they feel elated. They feel great. They feel special. And they want to do better the next time.

It is a great morale booster, but do not make it a habit because then praising constantly loses its luster, and loses its meaning. Moreover, children might start expecting it every time they do anything new, which later on can become counterproductive.

But definitely praise them when they do something good for it instills good behavior in them. They get to know that, if they do something good, they will be appreciated. Thank them when they help you cleaning the house, for example, or when they do well in school. And when you praise them, use positive phrases like:

- Wow, that was good.

- Good job son or good job, my dear.

- You are wonderful.

- You are amazing (or that was amazing).

- Thanks for the help dear.

- That is a good idea. I love it.

- We are/I am proud of you.

- I heard that you are doing well at school. Nice. I am so happy.

- Your teacher said good things about you. That made me proud.

When kids are appreciated for something, they not only love it and feel proud but are also filled with a feeling to do better. In short, they feel encouraged.

Remember how proud you felt when your teacher wrote something good in your school book or report card. You would show it to everyone around. Then you wanted to do better. You wanted to get the same kind of remarks in other subjects too.

If you are busy when they come to show you something, don't just turn them away. Take a minute and appreciate them. If you are really busy, then let them know that you are busy and will be with them in 10 or 15 minutes (whatever the case may be). Then when you are free, make sure that you fulfill your promise of talking to them and see what they want to show you. They will feel important and not left out. And if you have two or more children, do not keep appreciating one child and ignore the others. The other kids will start hating you and their sibling for that. Remember, whether it is how often to offer praise and for what or how much you spread your praise around amongst your children, the right balance is important.

# Chapter 14: Comparison

On this subject, people have many different opinions. It is a human nature to compare things. However, I do not think it is healthy to compare your children with other kids. I personally do not like to compare my children with other kids. I have two sons and they have some similarities but in certain things they are also quite different from each other. That does not mean that one is better than the other. They each have certain strong points, and they are both smart in their own way.

If you ridicule your kid, giving an example of how he should have acted by mentioning another kid, he may not become like the other kid but he will definitely feel belittled. By doing that, you are making your child feel inferior to other kids or his siblings. Remember, everyone has positive, and negative traits and so anyone can be criticized, but a child can develop an inferiority complex if you compare them with other kids. It brings negativity into their lives. They will begin to feel small.

Some kids may be strong in athletics and not so good in their studies or vice versa. Some kids are good at most of the things they do. Your neighbors' kid may be an excellent basketball player and be good in studies, or some other kid in your neighborhood may be good in soccer or with computers, and so on. When you see your kid not doing so good, you get frustrated or stressed, which is a human nature, but you need to understand that every individual is different. It is not right to compare them.

# Chapter 15: Character

**Character counts.**

Early in our life, we were taught by our parents: If you lose money, nothing is lost. If you lose health, something is lost. BUT if you lose your character, everything is lost.

So, think about it. It takes a lot to build character in your children, and it takes very little in the way of not paying heed to their actions and what you have built is lost.

For example, there might be parents who do not care if their child picks up something from a store without paying. They will look the other way. They do not realize that they are teaching a wrong lesson to their kid. In reality it is a small loss for the business but a big loss for the parent and the child. By looking the other way a parent is condoning a child's wrong behavior. It is also a sort of encouragement from the parent if the parent does not correct the kid right there. The child will feel that it is okay to steal if you don't correct him. In fact, if you don't reprimand him, he is learning his first lessons in stealing. His next target may be his own house and his own parents. By not stopping him in the first place, you are leading him down the road to disaster.

I was once standing outside a large electronics store in the San Fernando Valley in California while talking to the manager of the store. I noticed few other employees and a security officer also standing nearby. All of sudden the manager excused himself and waved to these people. They got into action and right away arrested a teenage boy coming out of the store. I could guess right away what must have happened here, but I asked the manager and he said this boy had been coming to the store and stealing stuff, and today they had been following him since he entered the store.

This time they caught him red-handed. The way the boy was dressed, he seemed to be from a family of means, but what he did brings into question how he must have been raised. Maybe his parents did not pay enough attention and failed to teach him that it is wrong to steal. Well, it was too late for him to understand. Now this young boy was probably going to jail, which could put a black spot on his resume. And indeed, building character in your children is an important factor to help them be good human beings but also to be successful in life.

You have to build a strong foundation to make a sturdy building. For building a strong base and character in your children, you need to teach them:

- Be good to others.
- Be fair to others.
- Do not cheat others.
- Do not steal.
- Be reliable and dependable.
- Be responsible for your actions.
- Do not blame others for your mistakes.
- Be punctual.
- Respect other people's time.
- Keep your promises.
- Be honest.
- Do not deceive others.
- Have strong integrity.
- Be trustworthy.
- Treat others the way you want to be treated.
- Be impartial.
- Do not offend others.
- Do not take undue advantage of others.
- Do not be mean to others.
- Be kind to others, especially the old, sick, and needy.

- Help other human beings.

- Never intentionally hurt others.

- Educate yourself.

- Be disciplined.

- Be confident.

- Do not procrastinate.

- Be diligent in whatever you do.

- Think before you speak, as your words can hurt others and you also.

- Do not bow down from your failure. Learn from it, then get up and start again.

- Do not fret or cry over spilled milk.

- See the big picture in life.

- Be grateful to the Almighty for everything and thank Him for a new day in your life.

Let me relate another wonderful incident that happened recently. It was Dec. 12, 2013. I stopped at a convenience store in Northridge, CA to buy a lottery ticket. As I asked the store clerk to give me the lottery ticket, I placed a 10-dollar bill on the counter. By mistake, I dropped that bill on the floor and went to get something near the counter. When I came back to the counter, this young kid waved the 10-dollar bill and jokingly asked me if he could pay with it. I was little confused, and then I realized that it was my $10.00. I laughed and told him he was welcome to use it, but he said no. He said that it was my money and he could not accept it. I was impressed. I asked his name and promised that I would definitely mention this incident in my book. He did not give his full name, just Robert. But kids like him are proof that there are people who are teaching their kids an ethical way of living and showing them the right path.

And this is the kind of character you want to build in your children. Along with that boy Robert, I would like to thank his parents who were certainly instrumental in teaching him the right lessons. We need more parents to show their kids the right way of living.

# Chapter 16: Teen Sex

As children go through the physical and emotional changes of puberty, they want to know about sex. They want to experiment with it, and that is part of a natural process. Though they may get some education about sex through their friends, school, the internet, and etc., but they may not be truly informed. We may live in an open and educated society, but as parents, it is our responsibility to educate our children about sex, especially issues relating to early sex.

Did you know that, in the USA, one in every four children is born without the couple being in wedlock, and most of these mothers are in their teens? In fact, there has been an increase in single-parent families in the last two decades, and mothers head most of these single-parent families. Most of these mothers have no proper schooling, and so they cannot take good jobs and most make minimum wage. As a result, most of these mother-oriented single families are living in poverty, and for that reason, most children from such families do not have healthy lives.

Many such families are forced to live on public assistance to cover the basic needs of food and shelter. And the financial problems for these families, especially for single mothers, lead to depression and nervous breakdowns. We see this every day around us, but we do not acknowledge this fact, and consequently, this big issue is engulfing our society.

Dr. Mihalas emphasizes the negative effects of teen pregnancy. Schools often do not have good programs for teen moms, and teen pregnancy puts lots of pressure on a kid as the school, peers, parents, and society initially reject her. The question "How could she do that?" always appears. She further mentions that, if a person has a good support system in the form of family, friends, mentors, and peers, life can get easier for the teen. Her family and support group can take care of her child while she continues her education. However, this is obviously not usually an option given the statistics.

More likely it is a scenario like this: A girl gets into a relationship at the tender age of 14 or 15, and because of unprotected sex, she gets pregnant. She was studying in high school, but now, she may have to skip school and miss a full school year. Her peer group may look down on her, or she may even lose respect within her social group. She may even lose good friends who no longer want to be associated with her.

Once she gives birth to the child, for some time there will be a kind of excitement for the new arrival into the world. But after a few weeks of that, reality sets in. Now she has to support the newborn. She looks around for help. In some cases, the girl might be able to leave the baby with her mother or some other family member for a few hours. In other cases, even that is not possible. And just imagine what kind of jobs would be available to a 9th or 10th grader, 15 year-old girl. They will be just the basic jobs with minimum salary. Do you think it will be enough to make ends meet for her?

In this situation, if her partner was also a high school student, what kind of income can he generate to support her? If he comes under pressure, he may also have to take up a part time job to support her. Again, in most cases, what kind of job would he be able to get?

After a while, frustration starts mounting between the young couple. Their love, which actually was infatuation, goes awry when problems get in the way. Now it is about responsibilities, because with children come responsibilities. There may be the arguments like this between the two:

Girl: "Can you take care of the baby tomorrow when I have a class?"

Guy: "Who me? I don't know anything about taking care of babies."

Girl: "Do you think I know anything about it? But still I am doing it."

Guy: "Oh, oh, oh. Don't get me into this. You should have thought about this before." It is not my job to take care of the kid.

Or it might go like this:

Girl: "Hey, Can you take care of the baby tomorrow? I have an important class."

Guy: "Hell no! I have a class too."

Girl: "Then who will take care of the baby when I go to school?"

Guy: "Well, babe, I have a class too."

Girl: "So, who will take care of the baby?"

Guy: "You are the mom. It is your responsibility."

Girl: "Are you crazy? Isn't the baby your responsibility too?"

These scenarios represent two people in their teens who were once so excited about being together that they did not want to be separated even for a few hours. They even dreamed of each other when not together, but after only a few moments of enjoyment, and being a little careless, their whole life changes.

After few months together with all these issues, their young minds cannot take it anymore. The result most likely is a separation. Now the girl wants child support because (of course) she cannot handle the financial aspect of being a single mother. The guy (in most cases) wants to get away from the problems, but it is also an issue for him to pay child support. In most cases, he does not have any income, which makes this yet more problematic for both parties.

If as a parent you fail to teach the children about the potential issues and repercussions of early sex, it may come back to haunt you in the form of all these problems because, when this situation arises, you have two choices. You shirk your responsibilities or you offer to support your children and help them. This whole scenario changes your life too.

Either way, you will suffer, however. If you don't support them, it may hurt you internally (sub-consciously), and if you decide to support them, it may hurt you financially and otherwise because you will have to make sacrifices socially and financially.

Some surveys indicate that teenagers used condoms for safe sex in the 1990s because, at that time, there was a big issue about AIDS; but lately they have been avoiding condoms. A study of a Canadian Sex Information and Education Council stated that more than 50% of sexually active students do not use condoms, so in other words, they are having unprotected sex, which indicates the size of the problem we face as parents convincing our children that the potential downside is real.

But we need to convince our children that, if they have unprotected sex and have a child as a result, later in life when they see their peers from school or college who are much more successful and ahead in life than they are it can really hurt them emotionally. They will inevitably compare how they had to take care of their kids and how their peers (now successful) take care of their kids providing not only all the things they need but doing so while living in comfort.

I am not saying that not all single parents fail to raise their kids in the right way. There are numerous stories of parents who have done remarkably well raising their kids singlehandedly. They became very strong and responsible parents in tough circumstances. In all honesty, however, there are always some exceptional people in the world who are willing to fight against all odds. But how many people are there like that? According to the statistics, most single parents are either living in poverty or just above the poverty level.

So, don't let this happen to your children. If we have made some mistakes in life, we don't want our children to repeat those mistakes. Show them the path from your experience. Educate them. In fact, Vandana Kumar suggests educating them about abstinence as a choice. Educate them to keep away from sex until they have completed their education and started their career.

# Chapter 17: Drugs

It's important to recognize and acknowledge that drugs have regrettably become a significant part of the American society. But to recognize the presence of drugs is not to accept the idea that, since they are so ingrained in our communities, our children will inevitably become involved with them. It's possible to live in the world but not be a part of it. This chapter will present some ideas for helping you deal with the problem of drug use and the possibility of your children becoming involved with them.

It is easy to see that the problem of children using drugs has reached a crisis level in our country, and if we don't find solutions soon, drugs could literally destroy our civilization. The only way that will truly work is to strengthen families when it comes to drugs, and in order for families to be so strengthened, parents need to take the lead. That seems like an obvious statement, but I believe parents are often the least informed about the subject of drugs. They most often have a good deal less information than even their children, whether their children involved in drugs or not.

Virtually every child in the United States of America today has access to drugs. If they want drugs, they know where to go and who to see. It may be that they don't know the specific person who will supply them but they know how to go about finding that person. If parents don't recognize the fact that their children have access to drugs and can find a person to supply them if they choose, they're naive at best and foolhardy at worst. In short, there is nothing you can do in to prevent them from getting drugs if they so choose.

It's also important to know that all drugs are dangerous. This may sound overstated. Some will say that drugs *can* be dangerous, but that's not true! I repeat, they *are* dangerous! To deny the fact that *any* and *all* drugs *are* dangerous is asking for potential disaster! And when I say *all* drugs are dangerous, that includes cigarettes, alcohol, prescription drugs as well as so-called street drugs. It's true that the effects of some are worse than the effects of others, but drugs are *all* dangerous.

Any substance that affects our moods, our emotions, our way of doing things, our physical sensations and responses, is especially cause for potential problems. This includes drugs that are prescribed to fight specific diseases, or infections, or sleeplessness or pain, or fatigue, or sexual arousal, or depression, or anxiety — anything we want to change in our bodies or minds fits into this general statement. That's because, when we start feeling better and that feeling is directly attributable to a substance we have taken, there is a physiological as well as a psychological effect that takes place and we tend to want to experience the same good feeling more and more often.

A conscious effort must be made in order to avoid doing what feels good when possible, or negative consequences can result. Parents tell their children this all the time, but often they do not present a very good example. The very best teacher, I believe, is the good example of a loving, caring, responsible parent. So, with respect to drugs, it is best to live the example of what you advocate, including the avoidance of drugs that are "socially acceptable."

## In Specific Terms, What Is the Problem and How Big Is It?

It's rare for children to become immediately drug-dependent from one-time use, but there are certain drugs that have this capability. Most often, children must be led up to the more rapidly addicting substances. They begin with slower acting drugs such as tobacco and alcohol, and in today's world, they may even get addicted to so-called energy drinks! Then they progress to the next level of drugs, which are quicker acting. There are four definite stages of drug usage. These stages are: *curiosity, experimentation, dependence,* and *premature death.* They're progressive and hierarchical, which means it is not possible to go back to a lower stage such as curiosity once a child has progressed to a higher one like dependence.

The next stage after dependence is *premature death.* There is sufficient evidence that whatever the substance, legal or illegal, it will lead to eventual premature death. Some drugs take less time than others but the ultimate outcome is absolute.

## Curiosity Stage

This is the stage where you as parents have the most influence. The further into the stages a child goes, the more difficult it is to get them back to where you want them to be, total abstinence. In this stage, children are most likely to communicate with you than in the following stages. It might begin with questions such as: "Why is pot (or weed or grass or whatever term is currently popular) so bad?" or "How come the police spend so much time chasing drug users when they could be going after real bad guys?" or "I know some dudes who use; are you saying they're all bad?"

The *way* you deal with these and other similar questions is very important. Lots of parents become extremely worried just hearing such questions from their children. In fact, frequently parents just want to avoid this kind of conversation. Some parents begin by attacking instead of listening, like the questions themselves must be aggressively dealt with or their child will be more likely to begin experimenting. It's a scare tactic that children immediately pick up on and it goes a long way in convincing them that their parents will not be reasonable and just answer the question. Parents are quick to be defensive and very emotional as if this approach will be more effective in getting children "back on track," but at this point it is overkill and kids recognize it for just what it is.

By going down that path, Dad and Mom lose a lot of credibility with their children and actually influence them to seek answers from others who seem more reasonable. Lots of times those they see as more reasonable are likely to give them the wrong answers, ones you don't want your kids to hear. So, to be forewarned is to be better prepared for the challenge.

Effective communication is a key! Keep communication open by speaking calmly and matter-of-factly. If you do not do that you will probably have given them a shove in the wrong direction. Answer their questions forthrightly, even if it seems a stupid question to you, as no question is stupid. Be honest but not dramatic. Reiterate your *good reasons* for abstaining from drugs and don't repeat the horror stories you've heard about drug addiction. Include the fact that a life of abstinence, for you, makes you productive, healthy, and happy.

Convey to them that being in charge of your life is the only way you would consider going.

In the curiosity stage, provide your children with all the good reading material you can regarding the subject. Choose what you give them to read from the perspective of what will interest *them,* not necessarily you. Children like to be entertained and there is a lot of literature available at your bookstore that is entertaining as well as informative. And remember, contrary to what is presented in public service television ads, scare tactics are more often than not ignored rather than listened to — let alone adhered to. More often than not, such tactics are prone to backfire and make kids defensive rather than being helpful.

**Experimentation Stage**

It's wise to assume that most every young person will experiment with some sort of drug, even if it's only a highly caffeinated energy drink. However, it might also be cigarettes, alcohol, marijuana or something else that comes around. That doesn't mean that every child will, but I believe it is better to make the assumption that they will rather than they absolutely will not. If they don't ever experiment, continue to thank God for your blessings and you have not lost anything for your being appropriately wary. If you assume they will never experiment and then they do, you are most often ill-prepared to deal with what comes next. If you assume that your children will never experiment with anything, then you run the risk of inadvertently causing them to think that, if they make a mistake and experiment, you will not be open to communication and that you will probably be highly disappointed and judgmental.

Experimenting with drugs is a mistake and an error in judgment. That is why, as I mentioned in an earlier chapter regarding another issue, it is important to start teaching them at an early age to abstain. However, mistakes and errors in judgment can still happen and they can be rectified. Dependence is more than a mistake or an error in judgment, however. It is a major step in the direction of self-destruction. With few exceptions, a one-time experimentation does not cause dependence, but rather, dependence is caused most often by consciously repeating the choice to use or indulge. You want your children to even avoid experimentation, of course, and so you should tell them just that. When you are open with them in communication, you also expect them to be honest and open about the things they are doing when you ask them. Indeed you *should* ask them from time to time, and trust them to answer honestly.

Here's a major point: You want your children to be open with you. If they know for sure that you'll forgive a mistake, an error in judgment, and you'll still love and help them, then you'll be most able to influence them to avoid dependence. If they think they'll be disowned for experimenting, you're much more likely to push them into the next step of dependence than to help them. In other words, to overreact to their one-time can of beer will make them more likely to feel that you already see their mistake as a "capital crime," just as punishable as shooting up cocaine.

### Dependence Stage

If your children move into to this stage, there is reason for serious concern. Professional help is mandatory at this stage. This is when the user looks for times, places, and the wherewithal to use their drug of choice. Their life is progressively becoming governed by the habit and the desire to feel its effects.

### Premature Death

As strange as it may sound, some people don't know what premature death is. Simply stated it is the end of mortal life before it should end. Accidents and diseases cause premature death, but it's also caused by drug use, which is neither accidental nor a disease in the same sense as cancer, influenza, diabetes, etc. It is self-inflicted and is not contagious in any sense of the word.

Sometimes, you may hear an inane argument such as: "Well, I have to die some time anyway. Why not die enjoying life the way I choose?" This is nothing more than a nonsensical statement from someone who is suffering symptoms of depression caused by their irrational behaviour. In fact, death via the use of drugs is more like a slow suicide. Every human being has the potential to contribute to his fellow man in a meaningful way. One who dies prematurely robs not only themselves but their neighbor of their positive potential contributions.

## Dealing with Curiosity

Just as soon as children begin asking questions about drugs and their use, you will know that they are in the curiosity stage. The thing to remember to do in this stage is to be open and honest with all of their questions. Don't take the questions they ask in a defensive manner, and don't attack them. Moreover, do not avoid their questions. It is also a mistake to assume that, if your children ask questions regarding the subject of drugs and their use, it means they're using or even thinking about using. It's much more likely that, if they are asking you questions, they are not beyond the curiosity state because, if they were in the experimentation or dependent stages, it's almost certain they'd *not* be asking questions.

As is the case with previously discussed topics in this book, it is important to educate children about drugs at the right time, however. Don't wait until they ask questions before you begin to educate your children regarding drugs. If you wait, you may go without ever hearing the questions. Moreover, waiting for them to ask only hinders good communication. If you have waited until you hear the questions, it's likely that your children's questions are being answered by people you don't want to give them answers.

And of course it is important that you first become informed yourself on the subject. Don't let this book be the only one you read regarding drugs. As stated earlier, the only purpose of this chapter is to alert you to the problem, with the hope that it's not yet too late.

Be alert for the following signs:

- Changes in attitude toward you or other family members.

- A change in school performance.

- A change in eating habits.

- Increased irritability with most everything around them.

- A change in comments about authority or authority figures and comments about how "stupid" laws and police officers, teachers, school counselors, and coaches are.

Of course, these behaviors may not necessarily be a sign that your child has begun to experiment with drugs. Part of the necessary process of growing up is beginning to learn to form their own opinions and to challenge ideas. Therefore there will be some of this from all children. However, if it seems that more emotion is being displayed than previously, there's reason to talk, not argue.

One further sign must be mentioned here: A change in the amount of time staying away from family members, either in their room or out of the house. This is one of the more tell-tale signs that a child might be using drugs. When children experiment with drugs, they know that parents are not going to approve. Therefore, they stay away. If you note this sign in your child, make sure you sit and talk. But again, remember it is time to talk, to ask questions and calmly offer advice, not to argue.

# Chapter 18: Role Model

Everyone has role models in their lives, that is people who have helped in shaping a person's future. Consequently, it is very important who a person chooses for a role model as it can affect their whole personality in different ways. We all choose our role models as we grow, as in fact quite a few people in our lives impress us and we try to emulate them. The first role model in our life may be our parents, grandparents, or other family members. Our next role models might be some of our teachers. Then, as we start studying and are more exposed to different things in life, we may come across someone else we admire and look up to. It may have happened that the people we admire or tried to emulate at a very young age might have disappointed us later on, but we continue to seek out role models to fill their shoes. But it always remains important what kind of person we make our role model as that choice is inevitably shaping the kind of person we are going to be in future.

Now, let us get back to our first role models, parents. If these role models have positive traits, it helps the child bloom in the right way, and if they have traits that are more negative, then there is a better chance the child will go in a negative direction.

Children look up to their parents for different things, but for every child, his father is very strong and can do anything. Have you heard that saying "my dad can beat your dad"? Children make that illusion in their minds about their parents because, for them, their parents are everything. In their minds, everything about their parents is good.

Unfortunately, they may feel hurt when they see that illusion breaking. They feel hurt when they see their role models doing something wrong. And when that illusion breaks, they look elsewhere for a role model. They might find the second role model in a particular teacher, or their role models could be selected from famous successful people like businessmen, leaders, athletes, people from the entertainment industry, or sometimes even people from the wrong side of the law.

Distinguished business people, leaders, or athletes most of the time impact those who consider them role models in a positive way. A child looks up to them as a towering person or personality and tries to be like them. In this case, there are strong chances that the child gets on the right track, as he is looking at the strong and positive side of his role model.

Parents should find out from their kids who their role model is, and in the case of some famous role models who are worthy of their respect, it is very important for parents to reinforce to the child that he can become successful just like his role model. I have heard about people who put up life-size portraits of their children's role model in their room to reinforce that thought process for the child. It helps the child tremendously. If you read the biographies of successful people, you will find this fact in many cases.

In my opinion, television, cinema, and music are slowly changing and shaping people's behavior and personality. There are different opinions about this assertion, and in fact social critics have been vocal about the pros and cons. But it stands to reason that, because things have changed at a rapid pace in the last few decades, and because of the subsequent drastic changes in music, television, and movies, our children are being subtly molded by these influences and in a negative way. For example, as I mentioned in an earlier chapter regarding stories, song writing, and music, not that long ago all were based more on love, mysteries of life, and some action. Now, all of these are more about sex, drugs, violence, killing, and the paranormal. The songs are more sexually oriented and focused on so-called ghetto expressions (with all the cuss words imaginable, and for some people, unimaginable).

If our child is watching these products, and he starts liking a singer or actor who is rich and famous, he may start idolizing him. This idol of your child may be openly doing and promoting drugs, violence, and killing, having sex with anyone and everyone, and so the child may want to follow his example. You can imagine the future your child may have in this case.

You can chart a future for your child by making sure you educate your child that not everything they see and hear is from actual life.

What is found in electronic media is all very artificial. Bill Gates has said in this regard, "Television is not real life. In real life, people actually have to leave the coffee shop and go to jobs."

As parents, it is your responsibility to educate your children that sports people, leaders, and successful business people are successful because they worked hard pursuing their goal whereas it is different in the case of television and movie actors. A character playing a negative role in a soap opera may be a fantastic and very positive person in real life, and an actor in positive role could be a completely negative person in real life. It is a fake world they inhabit on screen and so your child can't know who they really are from the roles they portray. So, they have to choose their role model in a right way, and for this you may have to help them.

# Chapter 19: Career

Every child has different traits, personality, choices, and the way he works. Each has different likes and dislikes too. Your one child may be very good in mathematics and the other may hate it. One child may be interested in accounting and the other in medical science.

As a parent, it is important to heed what your child is interested in, for based on your child's interests you may be able to guide him to start planning to choose a career. Children need guidance in charting their path, and as a parent it is our responsibility to show them the right path.

For example, if your child is good with numbers, he may be able to do very well in a career in accounting or some other field that has to do with numbers. However, if he is street smart, he may do well in sales or by being an entrepreneur. What you suggest to him depends on the child's nature and interests.

It is important to start taking an interest in what they are excited about when they are in middle or high school to see which direction they want to go. You can consult their teachers about your children's strong points. The suggestion here is that teachers usually know more about them as they interact with your children regarding academics more than you do and so they may see something in your child that you may fail to see. In fact, you may want to start interacting with their teachers right from the beginning.

You may think that it is too early to consider their career when they are just in their teens, but do not forget, "time flies." Before you know it, they would be out of high school, and then you will be scrambling to see what courses your children should take in college. If your child has not thought about it either, you will be clueless together at that time. This may result in taking the wrong subjects or prerequisites in college and wasting precious time.

As noted previously, choosing a career depends a lot on a child's personality, their interest in a particular field, their personal choices, their natural talents, their aspirations, the lifestyle they want, and how much money they want to make. And admittedly a lot of these questions will be hard to answer when they are barely 13 or 14 years old. Even if they have the answers, they may not be practical. However, it can give you some idea, and based on that, with your experience and knowledge, you can guide them properly. Even if you can guide them to some extent at that time, it will be better than not trying at all.

If you are unable to guide them in regards to their future career, then seek out professional help, like speaking to their school counselor. You might also go to the local library to check out books about the subject of career guidance, and of course the internet has a wealth of information. However, the important thing to do is to discuss a possible career path with your child.

You must remember that, although he may be inclined to go into some particular field when you first speak on the subject, he may change his mind completely by the next year. You may think that your child cannot make up his mind, but that is completely fine. Don't we all change our minds often even when making small decisions? One day we buy something and the next day we return it for some flimsy reason because we changed our mind.

One very important thing when you are guiding your children about their future career choices is to educate them about issues like indulging in early sex and the potential for problems. You may wonder what that has to do with planning their career, but if you return to the chapter in this book titled "Teen Sex" it will give you the answer to your question.

# Chapter 20: Money

Money is not the ultimate thing in life, but definitely it is a very important part of life. One cannot do without it either. You need money for anything you do in life, which is why we work so hard for it, to make our life better. Consequently, we need to learn the value of money, and moreover, it is very important to teach children the value of money. It is easier for an adult to understand the value of money, because we work hard to make our money. However, a person who has not worked for the money that buys what they need and want will not have that feeling.

That is why, when you go to the store to get something, your child will pick up anything that strikes his fancy and ask you to get it for him. When you say no, then he might start begging and crying and create a complete drama filled with a range of different emotions. If you become little weak and give in to his emotions, he feels elated, however. He has created this whole drama because he does not know the value of money, and moreover he does not know the difference between "want" and "need."

Actually our kids also learn from us when it comes to value, however. How many times do we pick up things from stores we really don't need? Your child may want another game, but does he really need it? It is hard to teach them the difference between "need" and "want" when he sees that you may "want" a new car but do not really need it.

Lot of parents wants to give everything possible to their kids on a silver platter. They want to give them what they themselves could not have. This is fine, but isn't this like a sweet poison? The kids will not value those things they are just handed because they are getting them so easily, material things like iPads, cars, and etc. They take them for granted.

If you teach them the value of money at this age, it will help them all their life. Teach them the importance to save from a young age especially. If they get into the habit of saving money at a young age, it may help them, and you, save for their college education.

To start with, get them an old-school piggy bank. Give them some small change every day or every other day and ask them to put it in that piggy bank. This way savings starts like a game for them. Ask them to put any small change they see in the house in their piggy bank and you may be amazed at the small treasure they will collect over time.

According to recent studies regarding finances, it looks like we are seeing a silver lining to the recession of the late 2000s in the way many of today's teens are handling their wallets. The so-called millennial teens have fewer credit cards compared to their parents, which shows the younger generation is not keen to get into debt and are embracing a thriftier lifestyle.

However, human beings have a very short memory about these things. Once the economy bounces back, lots of these young people may denounce their previously thriftier lifestyle and start splurging. It's true that we have to keep the economy going and so everyone hording their money is not in our overall best interests, but we have to take care of our finances too and see that we, and our kids, do not overdo things.

Money is a necessity of life, and can help a person live a comfortable life. But money can be a curse too if not handled in the right way. This happens mostly in homes where the parents give money to their kids without holding them accountable for their spending, which results in the child being irresponsible in terms of spending. Indeed, if not handled properly, an abundance of money can have adverse effects on one's life too. Children who are exposed to an abundance of riches and who are not taught to handle money end up in trouble because of it.

Moreover, an excess of money can have an intoxicating effect on a person. When a child is loaded with money, he thinks he is on top of the world, which can have an adverse effect on the attitude of that person and make them arrogant.

I remember in my college days, one of my friends used to behave like that. In our group, most came from well-to-do business families, but nevertheless our feet were on the ground. Most of the friends in our group used to help their parents after classes. Indeed, even the person I am talking about used to work in his family business. But perhaps because of the way he was brought up, he was arrogant because he was rich. Whenever we used to go to a restaurant for lunch, he had a habit of literally throwing money on the table in front of the waiters, treating them disrespectfully. You could see pure arrogance in his actions. Tired of this, one day we told him to stop doing that or we would distance ourselves from him and he may lose our friendship because he did not care about his fellow human beings. Slowly he started changing his ways, but it was still difficult for him to completely change his habits. Ultimately we learned that this attitude came from his dad, who had taught him that, when you have money, you can care less for others.

I have come across parents who just teach their kids that, if they have money, they can do anything. They do not tell them what is wrong or right. For them money is above everything, even above relationships or sometimes above the law too. They do not realize that they are sowing a poisonous seed in their kids' minds, which can poison even their own relationships later on. As they grow, those kids only see the importance of money and not anything else. For them money is supreme. Given that kind of an education, the chances are that they will care less and less about anyone else, and later on in life, perhaps even kick their own parents out of their home.

# Chapter 21: Values

A lot of kids nowadays do not know how to speak to their elders, which is indicative of a lack of respect. The words of respect, like referring to someone as Mr. George or Miss Tracey, are not used any more. Now it is "Hey George" or "Hey Tracey" even if George or Tracey might be 40 or 60 years older than the person addressing them.

During a recent trip, I was pleasantly surprised by the way the people in Bangkok, Thailand greet others. At the airport, wherever I went to inquire about something, they would get up and with folded hands greet me with *"Swadika,"* which means welcome, and then answer my question. Such a custom shows respect, which comes naturally to the people of Bangkok because their culture teaches them those basic fundamental aspects of dealing with others.

And we are not only seeing increase in disrespect but of the abuse of elders. Children should remember that their parents brought them into this beautiful world, and that they may have done so much to raise them, making sacrifices to provide their children with the best they could afford, to provide them an education, food, shelter, and so on. Elderly parents then do not deserve humiliation and abuse at their child's hand after doing so much for them. It is said that, as a person gets old, he again starts to behave like a small child. They start becoming dependent on their children just like their children were once dependent on them. And so I say to grown children, they took care of you when you were small and dependent on them, and so why can't you reciprocate? And if you cannot *respect* them, at least do not *disrespect* them.

Your actions are like a mirror to your own child. They do what they see. So it is extremely important to teach them empathy and respect for you by your actions toward your elders. If they see you abusing your elders, they will tend to do the same. In short, you have a vested interest in how your children treat older people because you will need their help one day and so want them to respect you.

Rather than treating an older person with disrespect because they are frail, treat them with respect because they have wisdom born of their experience. Give them your time and do not ignore them. Teach your kids to spend some time with grandparents. Kids can learn so much from them. Have kids entertain them. It is so much fun for both of young and old.

Grandparents love their grandchildren more than their own children. Do you know why? At the young age, a person has many roles to play. He gets busy making his career, building himself up financially. So, during that struggling mode of life, juggling with various things, a person does not necessarily notice and enjoy his own children as they are growing up.

However, when a person becomes a grandparent, he is most likely retired and his responsibilities are almost over. Now he looks at his grandchildren, who are a reflection of his children, and again he starts to relive those moments he missed as his own kids were growing into adulthood. So his grandchildren are now the most enjoyable thing he can imagine.

Don't take that away from grandparents. In fact teach your children about this fact. Your kids will love you all the more when you take your parents' place as grandparents.

Have you noticed that if you just open the door for some old person as a mark of respect and help, the person's eyes light up and out come the words, "Thank you. God bless you." Don't you love it? Again, we have to keep that tradition alive and pass it on to our kids. Otherwise, when we get old, we will be waiting for someone to open the door for us.

So, it is very important to teach them the basic courtesies like:

- Address older people with respect.

- Instead of calling them by their first name, call them Mr. or Mrs.

- Offer a seat to the old and sick if you are able and there is no other seat available.

- Help the old wherever possible.

- Take care of them.

Dr. Mihalas suggests that learning to respect others has to begin at an elementary level. The socio-emotional learning at school further reinforces the notion of respect for others. And because the role of school is important, you need to ask this question when choosing where your children will attend school: Does the school help a kid grow academically only or is it providing them with a foundation to take care of and respect their elders?

In America, we commonly put the elderly in an "old folks" home when they get sick. Since people often do not take good care of them or do not keep them at home, it is difficult for the kids to relate to the elderly. In other countries, however, grandparents are a critical part of the household. Therefore, kids learn to automatically take care of them and respect them. Kids learn from their grandparents.

Because this education regarding how to treat their elders does not necessarily come from home in this country, it is important for the schools to teach these foundational skills. Teachers should talk about the importance of empathy, helping others, doing good deeds in life, not offending others, to be honest, and taking care of the elderly, etc.

# Chapter 22: Manners

When a baby is born, there is all kind of excitement. We love him, hug him, and cuddle him. We show so many emotions naturally. Whether the baby understands it or not, we talk to him. In fact, however, some researchers think that the babies can understand what we are saying to them.

Once a child starts understanding the meanings of words properly, that becomes his own way of expressing himself. In other words, he takes his cue from us and starts speaking "our" language, whether good, bad, or ugly. So, if we start teaching him the words of respect and a nice side of language in how we regularly speak, then the child is going to adopt that language. On the other hand, if we teach him rude or terrible words, the child is naturally going to add those words to his vocabulary.

We may feel very happy when we teach a child some silly, or even cuss, words and he tries to emulate us. We laugh at the way the child says it, but what are we doing here, subconsciously? We are teaching something wrong to our child at a very early age. For us, it is just that moment, where we are trying to have fun, but the child is going to retain this word you have taught him forever.

Consider the following example: your child is four years-old and he hears you say the word "stupid." He imitates you, innocently repeating "stupid" in his cute baby voice. You laugh because it sounds funny. Although he does not know what it means, he thinks it is funny because you laughed. He will say that word again. If you laugh again a few times, then it may embed in his mind that it is okay to say that word. How do you think you will take it if he addresses you as "stupid" some time later? For him it will be okay because you unintentionally encouraged him to put that word in his vocabulary.

The same applies when teaching manners at an early age. We laugh when the baby does something silly. Okay, laughing once may be fine, as you want to enjoy those moments, but having him repeatedly do it and not correcting his behavior is not a good idea. By not stopping and correcting his behavior you are encouraging him to do this unacceptable thing.

Then, if he does the same when he is little older, that behavior will bug you and it may be a little late to correct him. However, you should correct him even then, as you should always strive to implement good behavior. Believe me you will be happy you did so at a later stage in their lives when you see other kids of the same age behaving not so nicely.

Addressing others respectfully is a first step in your child learning manners. People used to address others by saying something like, "Hi, how are you?" Now, it is something to the tune of, "Hey, what's up?" And it does not matter who they are addressing. They may be speaking to the person much older to them.

A few years back, a teenage boy approached me in my shop and asked me, "Hey, dog! What's up?" I simply asked him if he talks to his parents the same way and asked him to leave the shop right away. He got offended and left cussing. Again, this may well be the way most teenagers address others these days, but the first step in teaching a child manners is the *proper* way to address others.

From the very beginning it is important to teach your children the following:

- Be nice to others.

- Respect others and do not use inappropriate language.

- Wait your turn and do not interrupt when someone is talking.

- Do not display negative body language.

- Use words like please, thank you, may I, excuse me.

- Knock on the door before entering someone's room, and wait for an answer after knocking.

- Do not use abusive or cuss words. We are seeing this in our daily lives now. Even when just offering an otherwise nice expression about something, people use the "F" word and say things like "get out of here" just to express that they don't believe you. It may be fine when a child is amongst friends of their age group, but then it becomes a habit and they use the same expression even with their parents or elders.

- Do not make fun of people.

- Open the door for people, especially for the sick and elderly.

- Help people in need.

- Do not take things for granted.

- Do not grab someone's things without asking.

- If your parents ask you to do something, do it without grumbling or whining.

- Use good table manners.

- Use your utensils at the table in the right way.

- Do not indulge in showing off wealth or material things.

- Greet guests at home with a warm welcome. Give a hug to grandparents if they are visiting or if the kids are visiting them.

- Thank the host for their hospitality before leaving a party.

- Take care of and respect personal property of others.

- Ask for prior permission if you want to stay overnight at a friend's house. It is impolite and put parents in a fix if they just call from the friend's house at the last minute.

- Do not be loud with your conversation on their cell phone if they are in a public place.

- Switch off your cell phone when in a place of worship or at a bereavement.

- Respect other people's property and do not ruin it with graffiti.

# Chapter 23: Civic Sense

Litter, litter, and more litter. This is what we are seeing in the big cities. Let us consider few things wrong with our current behavior as a people and that can be witnessed every day:

- When some people go to the store for something to eat, they then throw the plastic or paper bag on the street, even if the trashcan is within reach.

- A person is smoking while driving, and all of a sudden they throw the cigarette butt out of the car.

- When you go to public restrooms, you see people spitting gum out or toilet paper is strewn all over.

Very soon, instead of a nice city, we will be living in a ghetto-like place if such behavior does not change. So, we need to discipline ourselves first so we do not engage in this kind of act, and then we need to teach our kids to have a civic sense that they enact in their daily lives. In short, if we want to keep our houses clean, we definitely do not want to make our city dirty.

Consider the following: you are on your way to work and quickly grab something to eat from a fast food restaurant, eating while driving. And then, because you are in a hurry as you going to be late and the boss will be upset, you don't look for a trashcan for the wrapper from the burger, the paper bag, and the empty cup from the drink. Instead, you just leave it on the street because, after all, someone will take care of it. Who cares, right? But what are you teaching your kids from such behavior? We see this every day, people leaving coffee cups, napkins, and small trash like that in the shopping carts, and on the streets. When their kids or siblings see this, they may follow them, thinking that it is ok to do the same.

Likewise consider this scenario: It has rained and water fills the side of all streets. There are motorists and pedestrians. Now, motorists technically and morally should be driving slower during and after the rain because there is a greater chance of an accident and because they will splash water on pedestrians and other vehicles if they are not going slow. But how many people have you seen following that rule? Again, if we do not have any sense of civic responsibility, we cannot teach our children the right thing.

Consider another instance of a lack of a civic sense, one you probably do not engage in but remains something we have to teach our kids to avoid. Graffiti is a big nuisance for society. Kids often ruin their neighborhoods with graffiti. Sometimes it is gang related and sometimes it is just that kids want to express their feelings and show their talent. However, they do not think that they are ruining someone's property and the neighborhood. We need to educate kids to respect other people's property. There are other ways to deal with their anger or to express themselves. If you think your kid is artistic, speak to their teacher and find a way to promote and develop his skills.

Education still begins in the home, even if you don't talk specifically about graffiti with your children. When the kids start writing, or I would say scribbling, they want to scribble everywhere in the house. They would scribble on the walls and the table and so on if allowed. On the one hand, we definitely want to encourage them to write and draw, but on the other they have to know they cannot scribble just anywhere. Get them a drawing book or a notebook and let them jot things down there. They will be more inclined to respect other people's property if you teach them to respect their own environment. This simple act of giving them an appropriate place to write and draw will help instill a civic sense they can apply to all aspects of their lives. Teach them from a young age about civic sense.

# Chapter 24: Dress Sense

Fashion is always changing. We will be bored, if it does not change and we have to keep wearing same kinds of clothes forever. We are humans, and like to try different things. Different colors, different designs, different patterns, and what not.

We see people in different costumes, some vibrant, some dull, and some elegant, and some, well... This aspect of fashion is what I want to talk about. When you see people wearing certain types of clothes, you say: "Wow, looks nice. Looks sharp, very elegant." But when you see some other modes of dress, you think, "How horrible!"

That is the difference. For a person wearing those horrible clothes, they are just cool, but for other majority of people, they are totally gross.

So, how do we define what is elegant and what is gross?

I feel that, if majority of the people say something, it does matter. For a person wearing pants sagging so far down his buttocks that he is showing his boxers it may be cool. However, who wants to see his underwear? For the majority of the people looking at him, that look will be gross.

We live in a society and not in a jungle. That is the reason, individually, even if we may like or dislike something, it may not be acceptable in the society because society has norms. So, where do we draw the line between individual expression and society's norms?

The line is decency. We need to understand and teach our children where that line is? We need to teach them the right way to dress.

Let us analyze it a little bit.

We can all see the amount of confidence it puts in a person when he is wearing the right kind of clothes, and we can see the difference in confidence between a smartly dressed person (be it a Marine, an executive, or a marketing person) and a kid wearing his pants down around his hips and showing his boxers. He has more concern about controlling his pants than anything else in the world.

There is a saying: "Dress for success." But now people wear anything and everything. They do not have any concern as to how what they wear looks on their body, even showing their butt cracks and what not. If the older people or parents are doing this, then what are they going to teach their kids?

Recently, I was watching a Latin show on TV. The host of the show was asking an obese young lady to try some clothes on, with the lady's mother sitting there. As the lady tried different sets of clothes, the host asked the mother what she thought of her daughter's attire. The mom started laughing and commented that her daughter looked like a big sausage in those clothes. Clearly the host of the show was making fun of that lady, and that lady was oblivious to the fact that she was being laughed at.

Have you seen some big people wearing such clothes that half of their body is trying to come out of their clothes? It is not that there are no decent clothes available for big and tall people, but some people just do not care how they look. If we are big and tall, we definitely can get the right kind of clothes for us. If we try to wear clothes that are three sizes too smaller, we will look funny wearing them.

How about people who wear slacks made of spandex? These slacks are skin huggers and become a part of the body. Have you seen someone wearing faun-colored spandex slacks? The person wearing them might think they are fancy, but does it look decent if the person looks like they are walking around naked from the waist down?

People may not say anything on our face, but behind our backs they do talk about these things. And the reason I brought this topic up is that sometimes it takes others to point out such errors in judgment to us, to correct the little mistakes that we have overlooked.

The same thing holds for our children. If they falter in the way they wear and look, thinking some absurd fashion is actual appealing when it is anything but, then it is our responsibility to guide and correct them.

# Chapter 25: Kids Manipulate

Today's kids are very smart. They know how to manipulate adults. In fact, kids today are smarter than adults when it comes to manipulation and will try all the possible ways to get what they want. They will try emotion (emotional blackmail), screaming, anger, threats, and crying. They would keep on trying until either they get what they want or they hear a firm no from you and thus feel that there is no further chance they will succeed in manipulating you.

This strategy, manipulation, starts at infancy. It is then that children start judging your actions, and based on those actions, they try the power of manipulation, and believe me they know which kind of emotion to use at any given time.

You have probably witnessed this firsthand. Perhaps when you have gone to the store with your children and they asked you to get something in particular and you said no, right away the tantrum started. They perhaps lay on the floor, held your foot, and screamed. No doubt, after looking around at all the attention your child is getting from everybody around you and feeling embarrassed, you may have gotten them what they wanted. If you succumbed to this pressure, they know very well which emotion to use the next time they are at the store with you and want something.

So, instead, do not listen to everything they ask for, but give it a thought and reason it out with them. You will find out that sometimes it's your experience and sometimes their logic which is talking.

I will narrate a small factual incident about Adi, a five year-old boy. Adi's dad took him to Target to get something. Adi tells his daddy, "Hey, Dad. Don't take me to the toy section. You know why? If you take me there and don't get me a toy, I am going to cry."

# Chapter 26: Make Rules

Every home should have some sets of rules. Define your rules and make sure that your kids respect those rules. That will make them more disciplined from an early age. They will not be able to manipulate you easily.

For example, some kids throw tantrums while eating because they do not like this or that. One day they like one thing and the next day they hate it. When dinner is made and you tell them what you cooked, they want something else. If you keep succumbing to their wishes, one day you will see that your life is quite difficult, that you cannot cope with all their demands. That is, the more you give in the more they want.

I remember my mother's rule about eating that all of us in the family learned at an early age. My mom would ask just twice if we wanted to eat. If we refused because we did not like what she cooked, she would simply say, "Thank you," and eat in front of us. Then, until we apologized, there would be no meal for us. So in this way she taught us to appreciate everything that someone has cooked for us. She would also have us say thanks to the Almighty for giving us the food in our plates.

Your rules should include, but not be limited to, when they are going to get up in the morning and who makes the bed after they get up. Once they are old enough, have them make their own bed and insist that they have to keep their room clean. If two kids live in one room, make a weekly schedule for them for cleaning the room, or they should mutually decide who does what and when and stick to it.

Help them the first few times with whatever chore they have been given. When you show them a few times how to do a particular chore, then they will understand it and do it accordingly. Examples include how to fold towels, how to clean their room, and how to set the dinner table.

Everyone makes mistakes in life. So, if they make a mistake while doing something, make sure not to get angry and instead, in a nice, polite, but firm voice let them know about the mistake. This way they will learn from their mistake and try not to repeat it.

If you do not make these rules, the kids will not understand their responsibilities, and if you punish them for not doing something, they will not understand why they are being punished. However, make sure not to overdo the rules for then your household becomes like a dictatorship.

Rules have to be followed in a right way, but the excuse of not doing something should be fine once in a while. However, if they know that they can get away from a particular chore by making an excuse, those rules will not have any meaning. Also, do not let them procrastinate about the things they are supposed to do because they will make it a habit.

There should be rules about the following:

- When to study.

- How much television they can watch or how much time they can spend on video games.

- How they are going to help their parents in household chores.

- The time to get home.

- And so on ...

# Chapter 27: It is That Simple

These are very simple guidelines to follow that can bring great results for you, your kids, our society, and the nation as a whole.

A friend of mine sent me a great quotation: "Why is it that everyone talks about leaving a better planet to our children…whereas nobody talks about leaving better children to our planet?"

It is not important to get judged by other people or society as a whole as a "Super MOM" or a "Super DAD." Just try to be a "Simple Mom" and a "Simple Dad," and once you do that, you will love the fact that you have achieved simple parenting yourself.

And remember the old adage: What goes around comes around. If you fail in your duties, it can come back to haunt you in the future in the shape of failure for your kids, failure for you, and failure for society. So, start today. Make some changes and bring some discipline to your family life.

Some people (even your kids) may make an argument about such discipline being a violation of their freedom. Of course, it is a free society, and we are proud to be a part of this free society, but the abuse of freedom is also wrong. Let me ask you: aren't we abusing this freedom? Please give an honest answer, and if you think it makes sense, then let us start today to mend things to make our house, our society, and our country a wonderful place to live in.

I understand that things can't change over night. In fact, these changes might take time, and a lot of time, but if we start doing things in the right way now, we may start seeing results in the very near future. Remember, a strong foundation makes for a stronger building. Just a little extra effort will make your children's foundation better, and in turn they are more likely to be a better person. Once they become a better person, the chances are good that they will respect you all their lives and will treat you well.

**So:**

Let us start teaching our children early in life by way of subtle counseling.

Let us start building a strong and friendly character in our kids.

Let us start making them more respectful.

Let us start making them more responsible.

Let us promise to give them a healthier lifestyle.

Let us make them more interactive in real life so that they do not become recluses living in a virtual world.

Let us teach them the value of money.

Let us teach them about the issues relating to teen sex.

Let us teach them about the issues relating to drugs.

Let us teach them about the predators around us.

Let us teach them about manners.

Let us teach them about developing a strong civic sense.

Let us teach them about developing a smart dress sense.

Let us educate them so that they are successful in life.

Let us help them with choosing a career.

Let us help them become good citizens of our great country.

Let us make a better future for our next generation to help you, the children, society, and the nation.

What are we waiting for? Let us start this wheel of change today, by just not promising to do so but by doing things the right way and fulfilling our duties from here onward.

AMEN.

www.ingramcontent.com/pod-product-compliance
Lightning Source LLC
Chambersburg PA
CBHW071904020426
42331CB00010B/2662